A Truant Disposition

RONALD GRIERSON

A Truant Disposition

Pages from my Diary

WEIDENFELD & NICOLSON
LONDON

British Library Cataloguing-in-Publication Data

Grierson, Ronald
A truant disposition: pages from my diary.
I. Title
354. 41006092

ISBN 0 297 81232 7

Typeset by Deltatype Ltd, Ellesmere Port
Printed by Butler & Tanner Ltd
Frome and London

I would like to thank my secretary of many years, Miss Hilary
Whiting, and various part-time assistants, Mrs Catherine Green, Mrs Terry
Joannou, Mrs Valerie Mottram and Mrs Wendy Wosterholme, for their
invaluable help.

Contents

Foreword xi

1 Behind Barbed Wire 1
2 On His Majesty's Service 5
3 At the United Nations 11
4 Footloose Banker 19
5 Rendezvous with George Brown 31
6 Tinkering with Industry 41
7 Afterthoughts 51
8 More Truancy 57
9 Bureaucrat in Brussels 63
10 Exit from Brussels 71
11 Business as Usual 77
12 The South Bank 87

Postscript 95
Appendix 97

For Heather and Jacob

A truant disposition, good my lord
(Hamlet Act I, Scene 2)

Foreword

THESE REMINISCENCES WOULD not have been written but for the encouragement of my friend and now my publisher George Weidenfeld. For years he has tried to make me believe that some anecdotes of my escapades into public service were capable of being turned into a book.

It took me a while to summon up the courage to put this flattery to the test. In the end it was the sheer incongruity of a relatively unassimilated German Jewish immigrant having a succession of encounters with that most intimidating of mafias, the British Establishment, which made me put pen to paper. Though I found it hard to bring myself to play their games, let alone abide by their quaint code of chivalry, the sheer polish of the Establishment's performance never ceased to fascinate me. Its mandarins have a penchant for 'safe pairs of hands' – the great and the good – and they feel uncomfortable with awkward fellows. I was never in doubt about my own place in this order of things.

I am sometimes asked why after more than fifty years of

association with Britain, including service in a prestigious regiment of the British Army, I still look upon myself as essentially German. I am not sure that I know the answer. Partly it must be due to the fact that at least half these fifty years were spent abroad. But it undoubtedly also has something to do with the fact that, while a United Kingdom passport which I am proud to possess alongside my German one makes one British, it does not give one the roots implied by Englishness, Scottishness, Welshness or Irishness. So I stick to my German or more precisely my Bavarian roots while never wavering in my loyalty to Britain.

What follows makes no pretence of being an autobiography in any accepted sense of the term. It is a random series of reflections on those periods of my adult life when instead of pursuing my business career I frivolously played truant from it. Each of these escapades had its fascinating moments and I would not have missed a single one.

I dedicate this book to my parents but for whose foresight my life might have ended in a concentration camp; and to my beloved wife whose wise guidance has prevented me from making even greater errors of judgement than some of the following pages reveal.

Mégève,
May 1991.

1

Behind Barbed Wire

MY FIRST ENCOUNTER with British officialdom was dramatic and inauspicious. It occurred on 18 July 1940.

Together with other Oxford undergraduates I had responded to a call to spend part of my summer holidays chopping trees in a forestry camp in Wales. The diversion of shipping to war needs had sharply reduced the arrivals of foreign timber at British ports and the authorities leant on the universities to supply undergraduate labour to relieve the shortage. We lived in a tented camp near Bishop's Castle in Shropshire, twelve of us to a large tent, and had our food cooked by charming local ladies. At about 8 o'clock in the morning of 18 July two constables of the Shropshire Constabulary walked into our tent, enquired after me by name and on having me pointed out presented me with an internment warrant from the Home Secretary under Article 18(B) of the Defence of the Realm Act.

Those witnessing this unusual scene included a number of undergraduate friends whom I was to meet frequently in later life, though at the time I knew them mainly as fellow foresters:

Roy Jenkins, later to become Home Secretary himself, Tim Cohen, like me a future banker, and John Lincoln, now an Australian High Court Judge and Vice-Chancellor of McQuarie University.

My arrest did not take me wholly by surprise. Article 18(B) had been much in the news and – though it was intended to apply mainly to British fans of Hitler and Mussolini and to non-refugee Germans caught in Britain by the outbreak of war – the emergency following Dunkirk and the fall of France left the Churchill government in no position to take chances. The policy was to intern first and ask questions later. My first reaction to being arrested was therefore relatively unemotional. Moreover, the police handled the matter with consummate elegance. After giving me time to pack my belongings and send the bulk of them back to my parents, together with a suitable message of my immediate fate, they took me to Shrewsbury police station. There two other detainees joined me and the three of us made the one-hour trip to our next destination, Prees Heath Internment Camp, in a comfortable police vehicle. Once inside the camp the full horror of the situation quickly struck me. Living conditions, again under canvas, were perfectly tolerable and the place seemed packed with graduate and undergraduate acquaintances from Oxford. But there was a tragic irony in being behind barbed wire at the very moment when I itched to join the fighting.

My wife frequently tells me that the lack of an early English education accounts for my inability to bear frustrations and to be what the Establishment admiringly calls 'a good loser'. She is probably right; yet no amount of self-control could in those circumstances have prevented even a less determined eighteen-year old from trying to move heaven and earth to escape from the frustration of imprisonment and join the fighting. Looking back on it from a distance of half a century I have to admit, as I was to discover many times in later life, that all this agitation proved of little avail. The outcome would have been much the same if I had relaxed and played bridge, the main distraction in our tent. After three months of internment my turn came to be summoned before a so-called Aliens' Tribunal. I was immediately given clearance and on 7 October joined the British Army at a recruiting centre in Shrewsbury.

But things had seemed very different three months earlier when we could hear and see the bombing of Coventry from our camp. I wrote frantically to everyone I could think of and asked my parents, who then lived with my maternal grandparents in Yorkshire, to do the same on my behalf. I still have copies of my father's correspondence with the Home Office Under-Secretary, Osbert Peake, with other MPs and with influential friends elsewhere. My own efforts were targeted principally at Lord Reading, a friend of my father's, who commanded the alien contingent of the Pioneer Corps and whom I had visited before my internment in the vain hope that he would somehow let me join his unit even though I was under age. Some of the approaches I tried in my desperation seem quite absurd in retrospect. Knowing that in the short run the chances of joining the British Army were slender – but that joining any allied army could secure release – I wrote a letter to an Egyptian fellow undergraduate whom I had known at Oxford, asking if he knew of a way for me to join the Egyptian Army! I never received a reply and heaven knows what would have happened had I become an Egyptian soldier. The fact that I wrote at all showed how frustrated and frantic I had by then become, and how unwilling I was to put up with even a temporary loss of control over my fate. To this day, as many of my friends have witnessed, I continue to find that rather difficult.

2

On His Majesty's Service

THE AUXILIARY MILITARY PIONEER CORPS to which a Shrewsbury recruiting officer posted me in October 1940 was not one of the smarter regiments of the British Army. Yet to an impressionable foreigner just released from behind barbed wire and anxious to play his role in the war it felt like paradise. Thanks, I suspect, to Lord Reading, my first commanding officer, I was rapidly promoted to the dizzy height of corporal.

Ilfracombe in Devon was the training camp of the Alien Wing of the Pioneers and I spent six months there before being posted to a unit. Our contingent consisted mainly of Germans and Austrians, with a sprinkling of Italians and a handful of men from the French Foreign Legion who had escaped to Britain via Dunkirk. In their honour a bevy of French professional ladies had made the pilgrimage to Ilfracombe and their favours were much in demand among all nationalities.

I spent the next two years in various Pioneer units, some engaged in forestry in the West County, others digging trenches for electricity, water and sewage in the Cotswolds and

Oxfordshire. (I still occasionally admire our work as I drive down some country lane.) The incredible boredom of our purely manual work was happily relieved by the presence of some highly entertaining characters, Arthur Koestler among them, in our ranks.

After much lobbying on my part (and a further appearance before an MI5 panel) I was commissioned as a second lieutenant and soon afterwards transferred to the airborne infantry, then known as the Army Air Corps. I did my parachute training at RAF Ringway and for the next three years served with airborne and SAS units in various operational theatres, first in North Africa and later in Italy, France, the Low Countries, Germany and Norway. A caring War Office, concerned to protect me in case of capture, had declared me a native New Zealander (apparently in the belief that fewer German interrogators would be able to trip me up on details of New Zealand than of say Yorkshire) and entered Christchurch as my place of birth in my personal papers. I did not at the time even know the difference between the north and south islands, let alone on which of the two Christchurch stood; so it was just as well that no German got down to interrogating me, even though in early 1945 I fell briefly into German hands. Having chosen my birthplace, the War Office left it to me to pick an Anglicized name. I forgot to do so and found myself still without one the night before my regiment was to embark for North Africa. That evening I dined with an attractive young lady, a goddaughter of my general's, at the Berkeley Hotel in London; we sent for the telephone directory and my dinner companion made the fateful choice for me!

Most of the military dramas in which I became involved have been better described by others; in any case their detail does not fit into the framework of these selective reminiscences. The main significance of my military life almost certainly lay in the fascinating insight which command of men in battle gave me into the nuances of the British character. I felt thrown in at the deep end of assimilation; in no other way could I have learned as much about my new compatriots so fast. Even now, fifty years on, I find it hard to reflect on the British way of life without subconsciously recalling those first days as a platoon commander in North Africa and Italy.

The end of the European war found me performing temporary office duties at the British Embassy in Paris, having been wounded in Germany a few months earlier. My task was to write citations for gallantry awards to French civilians who had helped us behind the lines at the time of the Normandy landings. Orders to proceed to the Far East were overtaken by news of the bombing of Hiroshima. In the new circumstances I was offered the choice either of immediate demobilization to resume my Oxford studies or of another twelve months in khaki as a staff member of the Control Commission for Germany, the quadrupartite authority administering the defeated country. This proved the first of many occasions on which my sense of adventure got the better of me. The sensible thing would have been to go back to Oxford. Instead I opted for a year as a uniformed civil servant in Berlin. My official title, bearing the rank of major, was liaison officer with the French element of the Control Commission. Other officers performed similar duties *vis-à-vis* the American and Russian elements.

One of our small practical difficulties was how to synchronize the working and eating timetables of the four nationalities. American officers started their day early but were usually ready to leave for lunch at precisely the time when the Russians, last to surface, reached their offices. When our American friends returned from lunch the rest of us were beginning to feel hungry and so it went on. This left only brief openings for four-power consultation.

I felt not the slightest kinship with the ruined Germany I encountered in 1945. Yet the physical spectacle of a devastated country, short of food, clothing and shelter and with tens of millions of refugees streaming in from the East, gave even the most vindictively minded among us an uneasy feeling of trouble to come. Feeding, clothing and housing this vast population while their own means of doing so lay in ruins had to be the most immediate concern of the occupying powers; and our work was complicated by the process of de-Nazification which left only relatively inexperienced men and women for the huge tasks of administration and management.

It was all the more surprising – indeed one of the paradoxes of the past half-century – that the Federal Republic managed to cope so robustly with the aftermath of unconditional surrender, whilst an earlier generation had found it impossible to come to terms with the consequences of the Treaty of Versailles. I am aware that as I write these lines a small shadow is being cast over this proposition. But even if the future proves more turbulent, the fact that for over forty years an economically dominant Germany remained one of the staunchest pillars of both the European and the Atlantic alliances – resisting all temptation to play one off against the other – is something none of us would have predicted in 1946. Berlin that winter was an unreal place, the occupying powers pursuing the mirage of four-power administration while no one had any real contact with the German population. The Control Commission, consisting of Generals Eisenhower and Koenig, Field-Marshal Montgomery and Marshal Zhukov, met once a month as a kind of pan-German cabinet. Their deputies, known as the Co-ordinating Committee, met ten days earlier to prepare Commission business. My task was trying to sort out differences between the French and ourselves before contentious subjects came up at meetings.

My main recollection of these early four-power meetings was of the easy relationship between the United States and ourselves, a residue of the closeness of the wartime alliance and a good omen for the future. Equally vivid are my memories, again a portent of things to come, of the utterly cynical stubbornness of the Russians and of the ludicrous touchiness displayed by the French to even the smallest of perceived slights. Some of the issues with which we then struggled seem arcane in retrospect. Much of our time was taken up with reparation claims by formerly occupied countries; we tended to get deeply involved in the detail of arrangements to ship dismantled German industrial plants to Greece, Poland and Yugoslavia. A recurrent theme in Commission meetings throughout that winter was how much German steel production the four powers would tolerate. The Soviet Union and France wanted it restricted to about 1.7 million tons per annum; we and the Americans were prepared to allow 2.4 million tons. The fact that a few years later German steel production easily topped 10 million tons underlines the unreality of our deliberations that winter.

In looking back on this, one tends to forget that less than a year had gone by since Secretary Morgenthau, one of Roosevelt's close associates, had put forward his plan for the permanent 'pastoralization' of Germany to prevent her ever making war again; and that at the time even those of us who felt that this went somewhat far still considered the destruction of German economic power not only a legitimate but also a practical objective. It was the golden period of our attempt to woo the Soviet Union into collaboration with the West; anything that could be remotely construed as pro-German was firmly stamped on for the benefit of the Russian connection. I remember an incident in July 1946 which illustrates this vividly. I was then a few months from demobilization and had been moved to a key military government job in Cologne. One of my tasks was to befriend Dr Adenauer who had recently and somewhat unwisely been deposed as Mayor of Cologne. One day I received a call from Noel Annan, a senior member of

Montgomery's political staff, asking whether I could persuade Adenauer to come to an informal meeting with him and Christopher Steel, then a Foreign Office adviser in Berlin and later our first ambassador to the Federal Republic. Adenauer was sulking in his house in the Siebengebirge without telephone or transport. I went to see him and asked him if he would come to such a meeting. He agreed moodily and a date was set for the lunch in my officers' mess in a Cologne suburb.

After much reminiscing about the past, Adenauer launched into a masterly analysis of the current situation in Europe in which two expressions – 'Western Christendom' and 'Occidental culture' – occurred frequently. It is hard to believe in 1991 that the utterance of these innocent words, now the common currency of Western politicians, caused all of us to develop doubts about the appropriateness of Adenauer being given a role in the affairs of postwar Germany!

I was demobilized in October 1946. I had risen to the rank of a lieutenant-colonel in the Black Watch, a position (not to mention the kilt it allowed me to wear) which my boldest dreams would not have conjured up six years earlier. The year I spent with the Control Commission had given me not only a rare insight at an early and impressionable age into the workings of government – for what we had in Berlin was a skeleton administration covering every field of public administration – but also a first-hand and rather disillusioning acquaintance with international diplomacy.

3

At the United Nations

ONLY A COUPLE OF YEARS were to go by before I had my next taste of public service. This time my employer was not the British government but the newly created United Nations Organization. I had returned to Oxford immediately after demobilization. Having obtained a not very grand degree (a special non-honours MA confected for wartime students) I left Balliol in mid-1947 for a job as editorial assistant at the *Economist*. My assignment was to help launch a new inside information bulletin, 'Foreign Report', the brainchild of the then editor Geoffrey Crowther.

In the spring of 1948 Crowther sent me to Stockholm to interview Professor Gunnar Myrdal, the famous sociologist who was then Sweden's Minister of Trade. Myrdal had aroused intense controversy by concluding a commercial treaty with the Soviet Union, highly unfavourable to Sweden, in the much-trumpeted belief that Western capitalism was headed for a 1929-type crash and that only countries which insulated themselves from this débâcle were likely to survive. I got on well with Myrdal and when some six weeks later – and to the undisguised relief of most Swedes – he was appointed Executive Secretary of the newly created United Nations Economic Commission for Europe he telephoned me in London and invited me to be his 'special' assistant. Once again, as in Germany two years earlier, the urge to try out a public function got the better of me; and with a bit of encouragement from Geoffrey Crowther – which I was vain enough not to recognize as relief at getting rid of me – I presented myself at the Palais des Nations in Geneva in April 1948.

The postwar tenants of that old League of Nations mausoleum were relatively unglamorous minor UN bodies whose meetings tended to be ignored by the media. By contrast – and as if to prove Oscar Wilde's theory that the dullness of diplomatic society is proved by the excitement invariably caused by the appearance of a new face – our arrival in Geneva was greeted with a great deal of curiosity by the press. Economic planning, sanctified by wartime experience, had not yet earned the stigma which attached to it later; and the ECE experiment was seen as a way of building bridges to the countries of Eastern Europe which had fallen under Soviet domination.

As we formed our team (soon to grow to more than a hundred) we made our first mistake: to think that what we did was of world-shaking importance. I later recognized this as an occupational disease of international bodies generally. In our case the clash between Myrdal's infectious enthusiasm for his new toy and the real world, focusing on the more important Marshall Plan then being shaped in Paris by a committee headed by Sir Oliver Franks, was guaranteed to give us a bumpy ride. The Marshall Plan came at an awkward moment for us and much of Myrdal's colossal energy was spent that summer and autumn on ensuring a role for the ECE in the new order of things. I was despatched to Paris to seek an audience with Oliver Franks and to try to work out some kind of collaboration. Franks received me very courteously but made no secret of the fact that the role of the ECE was not a subject which was high on his committee's list of priorities. Not accepting no for an answer, Myrdal went to Paris himself, taking me with him, to see whether Dag Hamarskjold, then head of the Swedish delegation to the Franks committee, would intercede on our behalf. Hamarskjold at first showed sympathy; but he later excused himself on the grounds that Sweden's original misgivings about the Western European response to Marshall had been satisfied. No one could say we had not tried. (I still have the telegram which Myrdal sent to Secretary-General Lie in New York desperately hoping to reconquer some of the ground lost to Sir Oliver Franks; it was a hopeless endeavour but Myrdal kept on trying.)

Myrdal saw the setting up of the ECE as the way to solve all kinds of postwar economic problems: the healing of the rift between East and West, the planning of industrial production across national frontiers and the making good by collective action of the raw materials shortages which plagued the economies of most European countries. Though my own mind was then still open to almost any economic doctrine, so long as it was well enough argued, the oversimplified way in which Myrdal and his team – including such redoubtable heavy-weights as the two Rostow brothers, Gene and Walt, and Nicholas Kaldor – set about blue-printing the future of Europe made me deeply sceptical about the value of economic planning; it also raised serious questions in my mind about the extent to which political objectives, such as East–West détente, can be achieved through economic holding of hands.

Like the UN itself, the ECE had no teeth. But like all toothless organizations, especially international ones, it developed an inordinate pride in itself and a determination to acquire power which successive setbacks did nothing to diminish. I encountered a similar obsession in Brussels twenty-five years later. We saw our job as nothing less than the construction of a European super-plan and we called meetings to deal with everything we could think of: steel, coal, railways, timber, fertilizers, sulphuric acid, agriculture, electric power, gas, housing and even the promotion of international trade. We also had a voracious appetite, as public bodies tend to do, for the services of so-called experts in whose wisdom we placed a touching faith. Forty years later the ECE still exists, bereft of the modicum of excitement which accompanied its creation, having accomplished relatively little, but also, one must admit, having done practically no harm except to cost the taxpayer a lot of money. In doing so, it has demonstrated another truth: that international bodies, once created, continue to exist whether needed or not.

My life in Geneva was interesting. Myrdal was a fascinating leader of a talented team; and I grew fond of him and our other colleagues, especially Walt Rostow who remains a good friend. Though I had reservations about the usefulness of our work, I could not help admiring the enthusiasm with which the UN's devoted servants went about their business of trying to improve the world. And I had fun rubbing shoulders with politicians and civil servants. Our plenary meetings produced set speeches rarely enlivened by anything memorable, let alone humorous. But I remember one incident, remarkable because a Soviet Ambassador displayed humour, at our first plenary. The delegates sat in horseshoe formation round an empty central area. The UK delegate was Sir David Waley, a senior Treasury mandarin. Bored with waiting for the interminable translations, not in those days simultaneous, Waley surreptitiously read a paperback thriller entitled *No Quarter Given*. During one of the translations, the book slipped off his knee and landed on the floor, title uppermost. The Soviet delegate, Ambassador Valerian Zorin (later to become famous in other posts) interrupted: 'On a point of order, Mr Chairman, I think the British delegate has dropped his brief!'

Myrdal decided that he must pay his respects to every European capital. I accompanied him on this whirlwind tour and only missed Moscow due to bureaucratic bumbling over the issue of my visa. Although the Marshall Plan had by then stolen most of our thunder, we were politely received everywhere and with some enthusiasm in Eastern Europe where we were seen as a much-needed window on the West. Two memories stand out from the mass of visits we paid. We were in Stockholm and due next day to visit the Norwegian government in Oslo. I had not realized that while Myrdal's big heart embraced all the world's races – white, black and yellow – this did not include Norwegians. Had I known it, I would have been less surprised when he asked me that evening to telephone the Norwegian Foreign Minister to say that he would find it more convenient if he and his cabinet colleagues came to Stockholm instead. I had to point out that this would create a major international incident and that he simply must not do it. Myrdal was nothing if not ingenious. He invented a bad cold and the visit was cancelled. With enormous difficulty I persuaded him to mend fences by reinstating it a few weeks later. But I had made the interesting discovery that even the most magnanimous of great men have their little corners of meanness.

Another memorable incident took place in London. Myrdal was the kind of fast-talking enthusiast whom any British government would find embarrassing. He hit it off particularly badly with Ernest Bevin who only met him once but on the basis of that brief encounter decided that the airy-fairy ECE was not for Britain and certainly not for him. When Myrdal paid his first official visit to London in June 1948, the Foreign Office reserved for it that exquisite mixture of surface politeness and behind-the-scenes rubbishing at which British diplomats excel and which left Myrdal totally baffled. Bevin excused himself on some specious ground from receiving him. Instead we were given lunch by his Minister of State, that splendidly extrovert Scotsman, Hector McNeil. Myrdal enquired why Bevin was so hostile to him. McNeil shot out the answer without a moment's hesitation: 'You've got it wrong, Mr Myrdal, the Secretary of State is not hostile to you, he just doesn't know who you are.' It was a monumental put-down and things were never the same again between HMG and the Economic Commission for Europe.

One of my senior colleagues in the Commission was Nicholas Kaldor, who had been a lecturer at the London School of Economics and later became Professor of Economics at Cambridge. Kaldor headed the research department, but played a far greater role than this position suggests. During the uneasy days when Myrdal attempted to change the character of the Marshall Plan, Kaldor and I were sent on a negotiating mission to Prague, Warsaw and Budapest. It was my first visit behind the Iron Curtain and Kaldor's first visit to his native Hungary since the war.

After two uneventful days in Prague (part of which I spent retrieving my passport which had become confused with the Archbishop of York's when we arrived on the same flight from London), we boarded the comfortable night train to Warsaw. Our programme, sent ahead by the Polish government, had us disembark from the train at seven o'clock next morning in Katowice, the headquarters of the Polish coal industry, to spend a day there before continuing to Warsaw. A few minutes before the train left Prague, the Polish Ambassador, a charming diplomat of the old school, appeared breathlessly at our carriage window telling us that there had been a last-minute change of plan and that we were now to continue straight on to Warsaw where arrangements would be made for us to pay a separate visit to Katowice by air a day or two later.

Happy in the knowledge that we could sleep late, Kaldor and I retired to bed. The next thing was frantic knocking at our compartment windows. When we lifted the blinds – at what we later discovered was seven o'clock – we saw to our amazement the entire management of the Polish Coal Board, led by their chairman, standing on Katowice station platform, wondering why Kaldor and I were not dressed and ready to disembark. Signals had evidently changed again during the night and we had to make an instant decision. Fortunately we obeyed our instincts which told us to follow the Warsaw instructions; but I shall never forget standing in my pyjamas alongside Nicky Kaldor at that Wagon-Lits window, both of us mouthing absurd apologies to our astonished Coal Board hosts as the train slowly drew out of Katowice station!

Our stay in Warsaw as guests of the Polish government left a deep impression on me. I had seen the horrors of German occupation in France and the Low Countries; they were a pale shadow of the destruction of Warsaw and the massacre of its citizens. The day after our arrival was All Souls Day; our hosts took us to the main cemetery on the outskirts of town where what looked like the entire population of Warsaw milled round the graves of relatives and friends. The graves themselves were of the utmost simplicity, with small wooden crosses, and stretched in long rows in all directions as far as the eye could see. Slowly, as night fell, candles began to be lit all over the cemetery. It was a sight I shall never forget.

A visit to Warsaw at that time was also an education in political realities. No one in the world understood Russia and the Russians better than the Poles; and no one had more cause to hate them. If they appeared to accept their fate behind the newly lowered Iron Curtain with equanimity, it was not out of love for Russia but because there was no alternative.

Our negotiations at the Foreign Ministry were painfully slow because they had to be conducted through an interpreter.

Suspecting that our Polish hosts spoke German (as did many Poles) we cautiously suggested a switch to that language. Our suggestion was badly received and we felt embarrassed to have made it. However, our embarrassment vanished next day when the Foreign Minister came forward with the brilliant suggestion that as we all spoke Swiss we could for the rest of our visit settle on that language!

One of Myrdal's pet ideas was to recruit a senior US industrialist to give credibility to some of our economic initiatives. In retrospect this was an absolutely crazy notion, betraying a naïve faith in the ability of a public body to promote industrial activity. Its origin lay in the success, in very different circumstances, of businessmen like Jean Monnet when they headed allied supply missions in Washington during the war; and I came across it in later years as I observed left-wing governments, dedicated to central planning, searching frantically for important business names to associate with their endeavours.

Much as I enjoyed my spell in this bastion of feverish activity, I decided in November 1948 to call it a day and start on my chosen career as a banker in London. The eight months I spent in Geneva gave me a remarkable ringside view of the international arena. It also gave me my first opportunity to visit the United States, though four days in an overcrowded building at Lake Success on Long Island can hardly be said to have given me the opportunity to gain a balanced impression of that great country.

4

Footloose Banker

LOOKING BACK, it seems odd that I gave up the thrill of a well paid and tax-free diplomatic job in Geneva for the relative boredom – in those pre-yuppie days – of a poorly remunerated traineeship in English merchant banking. It may explain why in later years I allowed myself to be lured back so easily to other forms of public service.

In the event quite a few years were to go by before that happened. I spent those years contentedly (and, for a large part, abroad) with one of London's merchant banks, learning my trade at the hands of one of its truly great practitioners, the late Sir Siegmund Warburg. Although I was enthusiastically committed to my City career I showed even in those days a readiness to succumb to outside temptations which a more single-minded devotee to banking might have resisted. The fact that I was financially independent – and not desperately interested in making money – presumably encouraged this tendency.

The first temptation, if it can be called that, came in 1948 in the form of a summons from the War Office. I was asked to accept a commission in the newly formed Territorial SAS which had been grafted on to an ancient regiment, the Artists' Rifles. My initial reluctance to be drafted back into part-time khaki, knowing how much of my spare time it would consume, met with a polite but firm reminder from the military authorities that a lot of money had been spent on my wartime training and that a refusal would not be kindly received. I was re-commissioned as a major to command one of the Territorial SAS squadrons and I held my commission until 1971 (although in 1952 I ceased to be active and was moved to the Reserve). For three years I spent several evenings each week in a gloomy barracks off Euston Road and devoted part of my summer holidays as well as many weekends to exercises on moors, cliffs and mountainsides. The only light relief was our regimental privilege of mounting the guard of honour at the Royal Academy on the evening of the annual dinner. The guard commander was by tradition invited to attend the dinner which entailed a lightning change from battledress to white tie in five minutes!

Another semi-military activity in which I became involved was the negotiation of British military awards to French civilians who had helped us in the resistance. A series of investitures – in Paris, Nancy and Rennes – were planned for the latter half of 1948; and awards ranging from the KBE to the newly struck King's Medal for Courage were to be presented by the British Ambassador. Obtaining the consent of the French –the responsibility of the Foreign Office – proved more difficult than we had anticipated, the French government insisting on vetting the political background of every individual before giving the green light required by diplomatic usage. The official at the Foreign Office with whom I dealt on these matters was none other than Guy Burgess, of subsequent Moscow fame. I doubt if this complicated the issue, but the French authorities proved very difficult over endorsing awards to known or suspected left-wing sympathisers; and since many of our helpers – and some to whom we literally owed our lives – came from that background we were forced to cancel a number of key awards. For years afterwards I received moving letters from French citizens unable to understand – or understanding too well – why some who had been prominent in assisting us were totally ignored. I found these letters tough to answer.

I attended the various investitures and thought them incredibly moving. Our own lives had by then returned to normal and 1944 seemed a long way off; but for our resistance friends the events and emotions of those days had lost none of their poignancy and it did us no harm to be reminded.

An embarrassing incident occurred on the day of the Nancy ceremony at a lunch offered in our honour by the Prefect of Lorraine, well-known resistance hero. Halfway through lunch the British Consul-General in Strasbourg, deputizing for the Ambassador, produced from his pocket a Foreign Office telegram outlining Mr Bevin's views on the Palestine situation, then in its tricky post-partition throes. Bevin's views were not conspicuously partial to the Jewish cause; and the Prefect was a distinguished member of the French Jewish Community. Lesser mortals might have hesitated; but our Consul-General charged in with a loud recital of the entire text. I shall never forget the spectacle of Christopher Sykes, one of our SAS colleagues, practically disappearing under the table in a vain effort to find one of the Consul-General's legs and kick it. Not content with one gaffe, the unfortunate diplomat, when reading out the citations that afternoon, got his monarchs confused and instead of saying that the honour was conferred by George VI referred at least once to King George III and several times to George IV. Unable to contain himself, Sykes was heard muttering audibly: 'Thank God, he's at least got the dynasty right.'

My subsequent escapades into the public sector were strictly non-military. The first was a call from Peter Thorneycroft, then Minister of Aviation, to serve on a committee set up to investigate the circumstances in which BOAC, the state-owned operator of overseas air routes, had come to lose a lot of public money investing in Middle East Airlines, a stake which Pan American had been only too glad to jettison a few months earlier. Our remit required us to make recommendations for the avoidance of similar mishaps in the future. This committee, presided over by the Chairman of F. W. Woolworth, sat for several months and heard evidence from all the grandees of civil aviation. We found more than a trace of carelessness and poor judgement in their conduct and made recommendations valid for nationalized industries as a whole. Most important from my point of view, service on the committee introduced me to three features of British public life which I encountered frequently in later years.

First, I learnt what a tremendous show Whitehall puts on even for those who serve it temporarily. The ink was barely dry on our appointments when an all-caring civil service staff sprang into action to minister to our needs. Secretaries held our hands on every aspect of our work: how to collect evidence, how to sift it, whom to listen to. I began to suspect that they had pre-drafted our entire report before we even held our first meeting. One could not help feeling thoroughly – and dangerously – cosseted by this warm Whitehall embrace. I also experienced for the first time the arrogance of the Establishment when forced to account for itself to those it regards as its inferiors. Peter Thorneycroft had chosen for our committee five individuals none of whom could remotely be described as Establishment figures. By contrast, we had to interview very powerful mandarins of the aviation industry who left us in no doubt as to how they felt about having to justify themselves to people they considered unfit to make such judgements. Finally, the spectacle of a large state industry floundering in confusion and inefficiency made me acutely aware of the vital role which competition and accountability to proprietors play in ensuring the best use of resources. It removed what little doubt lingered in my mind about the unfitness of the state to control what in those consensus days were regarded as the 'commanding heights of the economy'.

My next truancy was of a more colourful nature. In one of its unwise moves, my bank had invested in the capital reorganization of a British company owning the Peruvian railways. These railways, connecting the coast of Peru with the mineral wealth of the interior, performed vertical climbing feats normally expected only from mountain goats; equipped with ordinary locomotives and coaches, they managed to zigzag in a few hours from sea level to a height of 16,000 feet. This transport miracle, which also included boats on Lake Titicaca connecting Peru with Bolivia, had been conceived and built in the 1880s by an Irish engineer who persuaded the Peruvian government to borrow from British investors sums out of all proportion to the capacity of the Peruvian economy. Successive governments in Peru compounded this misjudgement by treating the railways as a source of livelihood for friends, relatives and constituents to whom they regularly awarded outrageous pay rises. Small wonder that the operation was a financial disaster from the start and that the lenders and operators never earned a penny on their investment.

My thankless task was to try to talk the Peruvian government into a more responsible stance. We had little luck and in desperation welcomed – sometimes quietly encouraged – the appearance of xenophobic articles in the Peruvian press demanding the instant repatriation at whatever cost of this vital national asset of the Peruvian people. But the nerves of the government of Peru proved stronger than ours and another twenty years of misery went by before the railroads were finally taken off the shareholders' hands without a penny being paid in compensation.

During my protracted stays in Peru I occasionally paid visits to the impoverished interior of the country. On one of them I was flown to an extraordinary encampment on the banks of the Peruvian Amazon. There a wealthy American foundation maintained an elaborate headquarters staffed by men and women of many nationalities and operating a fleet of small aircraft, all for the purpose of learning and committing to script the tribal languages of the Peruvian interior so that the Bible could be translated into them. It was an immensely costly operation and I remember being taken aback by this patent misdirection of a well-meant charitable purpose.

Another semi-public activity in which I became involved in the late fifties and early sixties was the creation of the Atlantic College in Wales. Dr Kurt Hahn, the famous German educator who had been Prince Philip's headmaster at Gordonstoun, involved me in launching his latest venture – an international sixth-form college with a heavy bias to leadership training. With funds provided by Antoine Besse, the son of the founder of St Antony's College in Oxford, we bought St Donat's Castle in Glamorgan, a magnificent medieval pile which had been expensively restored by William Randolph Hearst for his mistress Marion Davies in the 1920s but abandoned shortly afterwards on discovery of a noisy foghorn in the nearby Bristol Channel.

Acquiring the castle exhausted our funds. For the next two years we were engaged on a frantic campaign to raise money to equip it as a college and to condition the British educational establishment to its acceptance. The former was in the end achieved against heavy odds, the West German government playing a key role by providing £250,000 at a critical moment; and the college opened its doors to its first pupils in 1962. Conditioning public opinion proved a more difficult job. A major step towards it was a dinner at Claridges which I had been asked to organize and at which Prince Philip was to speak.

We managed to secure a remarkable attendance – church leaders, politicians, academics, educators, newspaper proprietors, editors and a cross-section of businessmen – and both Dr Hahn and Prince Philip made rousing speeches in support of the project. Unfortunately the third speaker, Lord Ismay, became indisposed at the last moment and in my eagerness to replace him I made the mistake of bullying a distinguished Oxford don, known for his witty oratory, into taking his place. My Oxford friend, Bill Williams, decided to punish me for my impertinence by larding his speech with unhelpful comments, saying that the Atlantic College reminded him of moral rearmament before 1939 when it was said to be good for the Japanese and that we would send our nephews there rather than our sons. It was a good lesson in what happens when one pushes people too hard to do things they would rather not do; and it set back our fundraising prospects by more than a year.

My next escapade made me the accidental 'discoverer' of the Costa Smeralda in Sardinia. In October 1959 I happened to walk down the Via Veneto in Rome when I bumped into an old friend, Johnny Miller, erstwhile bureau chief of the London *Times* in Washington. I asked him what he was doing in Rome and learnt that he had just returned from Sardinia where for a few thousand dollars he had bought a couple of acres on a remote beach in the Northeast and was building himself a small holiday home. For years Sardinia had been virtually out of bounds to tourists because of malaria; DDT had removed this handicap and people were beginning to take an interest in the island's possibilities. I asked Miller for the name and address of someone I could contact there and he directed me to the peasant in Arzachena from whom he had acquired his land.

It took me some months before I could organize myself to go there but when I did – a quite complicated journey in those days – I was immediately struck by the extraordinary beauty of the coastline now known as Costa Smeralda. Not only was it then totally uninhabited; it also lacked roads, water, electricity and any other form of infrastructure. Virtually the whole area was for sale but negotiations were likely to be difficult because ownership of each strip of land was shared among dozens of relatives many of whom had emigrated to North and South America. I decided to return a month later for a closer look. This time I came with a motley crowd of friends brought together by the accident of hearing of my discovery. We stayed at a primitive local inn and in the absence of roads had to inspect the land from a small motorboat rented from a local fisherman; the sight of such dignitaries as the late Lord Thomson, then already in his late sixties and immaculately dressed in a double-breasted suit and Homburg hat, and of the Aga Khan and his half-brother Patrick Guinness – all of them in our party that weekend – caused a good deal of local astonishment.

We felt like nineteenth-century colonial adventurers as we shook hands on a modestly priced purchase of some 800 acres of coastal land, some of it of incredible beauty and now the core of the Costa Smeralda. Our intention was to divide it among ourselves so that each of us could build a house. The first hurdle was to convert a so-called purchase into actual ownership. To this end I persuaded a solicitor friend of mine, Pat Hart, to spend several weeks in Sardinia, moving from family to family, to obtain the needed signatures. He accomplished this mission with distinction. Our next task was to persuade the Sardinian government to help us with the infrastructure. This gave every indication of being extremely difficult and at the end of two years we came to the conclusion that the project could only prosper in the hands of a major entrepreneur willing to invest a lot of money and to promote the project on a grand scale. The Aga Khan showed interest in this role and most of us sold him our land so that he could get on with what has now become one of the most sought-after – and I hope for him profitable –

holiday spots in Europe. Some of our original syndicate kept small pieces of land and fitted them into the Aga Khan's master plan; rather foolishly I kept nothing. I have often kicked myself for that.

In February 1962 I accepted an invitation from Lord Thomson – a man I greatly admired – to accompany him and others on what was billed as a high-level weekend visit to Moscow. The occasion was the first anniversary of the *Sunday Times* colour supplement, itself a 'first' in British journalism. It was to give me a chance to set eyes on Nikita Khrushchev.

The flight to Moscow in an eight-engined Russian aircraft was made memorable by my friend Whitney Straight, a veteran aviator, who spent the entire time explaining why eight-engined aircraft designs were an engineering disaster and had been abandoned decades ago by the Royal Navy. I took care not to sit anywhere near him on the return journey. I had never been to the Soviet Union before, and Roy Thomson arranged for me to spend the first morning with the Soviet Bank for Foreign Trade. I cannot pretend that this was an exhilarating experience but I was given (and still have) the Bank's prospectus in English informing potential account holders that total secrecy was guaranteed on all operations!

The highlight of the weekend was a sixty-minute interview with Khrushchev in the Kremlin at which Thomson and the General Secretary engaged through interpreters in a 'tour d'horizon' of staggering banality. Back at the hotel, the entire foreign press corps laid siege to Thomson to hear his account of the interview. I dined that evening with our Ambassador, Humphrey Trevelyan, and the Reuter tape reporting the press conference was brought in as we dined. I still remember Trevelyan's pained expression as he mentally measured the harm done to the delicate state of Anglo-Soviet relations.

My final and perhaps most important truancy from banking – if only because it was full-time – occurred in 1964, just after the election which brought Harold Wilson to power. Word reached me that the new Labour administration were about to ask me to do a job for which I had no stomach. Rather than have to turn it down I decided that this was the moment to carry out a project on which I had been keen for a long time – a sabbatical. It had always irked me that sabbaticals were the privilege of academics and were denied to ordinary mortals. To the amazement of my colleagues I accepted an invitation from Henry Kissinger, then head of the Centre for International Affairs at Harvard University, to join a Fellowship Course which Harvard ran each year for some twenty senior diplomats and service officers from NATO countries. The course started in October and there happened to be a vacancy; in spite of my lack of qualifications I was enrolled overnight and became a temporary Fellow of the Harvard faculty.

I had a fascinating six months delving into military and diplomatic topics under Kissinger's inspiring guidance. Sabbaticals are useless unless one spends them doing something sufficiently challenging in intellectual terms to take one's mind entirely off normal preoccupations. Harvard satisfied this requirement to an extraordinary degree. While at Harvard I was also asked by our Embassy in Washington to give pep talks on the British economy to senior businessmen in various US cities. I did not find this easy, given the mess which our political masters were making of things, but somehow the convention that when abroad one speaks well of one's country, whatever the facts, triumphed over my profound misgivings. I doubt if my listeners in places like Chicago and Los Angeles, among them many old business acquaintances, found me convincing. But my task was light and joyful compared with the hot potato handled by another London banker who was asked to sell the merits of George Brown's so-called National Plan – one of the most absurd documents ever to come from any government – to an audience of bankers in New York City!

My earlier contacts with the United Nations Secretariat also brought an invitation to go from Harvard to Bangkok as an 'expert' adviser to the Chairman of the Organizing Conference of the newly born UN Economic Commission for Asia. The Chairman, a charming Japanese banker called Watanabe, whom I had years earlier known as the Municipal Director of the city of Tokyo, made a great fuss of me but paid absolutely no attention to such advice – not much – as I was able to offer.

More important than anything else, my stay at Harvard permitted me to close a chapter of my life which had gone on too long: my bachelorhood. I had known the lovely girl who was to become my wife, Heather Bearsted, for quite a long time but it took the relaxed atmosphere of Harvard for a romance to develop. Two years later we were happily married in Washington DC. Thanks to Henry Kissinger I had acquired the best imaginable companion – and a glamorous step-daughter, Felicity Samuel, into the bargain – for the two major and rather controversial bouts of public service on which I was shortly to embark.

5
Rendezvous
with George Brown

IT ALL BEGAN innocently enough at a dinner party in Harold Lever's flat in Eaton Square in the spring of 1966. Lever was at that time an acquaintance rather than a friend – he has meanwhile (in spite of what I am about to recount) become a good friend – and the invitation to dine with him and his charming wife came out of the blue only a short time after my return from Harvard.

I remember arriving late and finding the other guests already assembled. Conspicuous among them – if only in their relevance to this tale – were George Brown, then First Secretary of State and Minister of Economic Affairs, and Arnold Weinstock, the celebrated whizzkid who had recently taken over and successfully revamped the sleepy old General Electric Company. Soon after dinner George Brown took Weinstock and me aside and without much ado invited both of us to join the board of the newly announced and highly controversial Industrial Reorganisation Corporation (IRC) which was to 'drag British industry kicking and screaming into the twentieth century'.

It was evident that Brown had treated himself generously to Harold Lever's excellent wines and both Weinstock and I realized that this was a time for caution. We thanked Brown for the flattering thought and politely pointed out some of the difficulties which the invitation presented for each of us. Not surprisingly, this did not stop Brown from rushing to the telephone and waking up his private secretary (John Burgh, now President of Trinity College, Oxford) to tell him that he had all but recruited us and would Burgh be ready to receive our final acceptances next morning!

The following day, after a quick consultation, Weinstock and I telephoned Brown to say that our respective conflicts of interests were such that we simply could not see our way to accepting. This was the end of the matter for Weinstock but unhappily not for me. A few weeks later Wilson announced a general election which he won with an increased majority. Shortly afterwards, Brown sent for me again and asked me whether the conflict problem which had prevented me from accepting his original invitation could be resolved by my taking leave of absence from merchant banking and becoming the full-time managing director of the new Corporation.

It was a difficult decision to take. I was far from sharing the boy-scout enthusiasm of the Wilson government for this kind of economic engineering; on the other hand, the decision to create the IRC was irreversible and the consensus among my friends and colleagues was that someone of my basically sceptical temperament might steer it away from the crazier adventures which our socialist masters had earmarked for it. I thought about it and a month later told Brown that in principle I was ready to serve as deputy chairman and managing director of the new organization. I made no fuss over having to resign from all my directorships but insisted on one condition: a free hand in choosing my staff.

The prevailing custom in the United Kingdom was for

businessmen accepting temporary appointments in the public sector to be 'seconded' by their businesses and for the drop in their remuneration to be made good by their employers. The idea of becoming a transaction did not appeal to me; I therefore severed my connection with my employers and – as is the custom in America – made myself available as an individual. I also followed this procedure on subsequent occasions.

The White Paper, making the case for the IRC, was a boring document full of woolly generalizations about the shortcomings of British industry and well-meaning advice on how the IRC could cure them. Taking its cue from Wilson's musings about the 'white-hot technological revolution', the IRC was to serve up the traditional menu of the corporatist state: the pursuit of size at almost any cost (the flaws of so-called economies of scale being as yet undiscovered); the achievement of industrial 'orderliness', i.e. the arrangement of industry on neat blueprints cosily negotiated with government and as far as possible eliminating competition; and, last but not least, the picking of 'industrial champions' on whom the blessings of government support could be quietly bestowed, at home and abroad, to the discomfort of less favoured competitors. The fact that these corporatist concepts clashed head-on with the essentially disorderly thrust of capitalist enterprise did not greatly worry the advocates of this policy.

Some went even further and saw the IRC as a grand holding company controlling the commanding heights of the British economy. To his credit George Brown was too realistic to share this view, but both Douglas Jay, then President of the Board of Trade, and Tommy Balogh, the Rasputin at Number 10, made no secret of such aspirations. Mouth-watering comparisons were made with IRI, the Italian state holding company, and I spent a good deal of time explaining that not only was IRI a creature of circumstances rather than a product of rational thought but that it had become a byword for inefficiency and corruption. This did not stop Labour ministers and their economist advisers casting envious glances in the direction of Italy: imported solutions somehow seemed better than home-grown ones.

From the start I never concealed my deep misgivings about the usefulness of the new organization and my general scepticism about the concept of government-led restructuring of industry. The IRC board of directors whom George Brown had handpicked from assorted industrialists, known for their pro-Wilson sympathies, knew and accepted that I would proceed gingerly and that I would not involve the IRC in projects which could be realized without our intervention. My line was that if at the end of six months we had not done a single deal we should regard this as a quite satisfactory outcome – proving that the British economy could get along without us – and that we must not allow ourselves to be panicked into action just so as not to have to report inactivity to Parliament.

Finding top people for the IRC staff proved difficult. I was determined to recruit bright young professionals with sound backgrounds who shared my view of the marginality of the IRC's role and could be relied upon to look at problems objectively rather than possessively. This disqualified a number of individuals from the academic world whom my political masters proposed to me. And some of the most suitable candidates shared my scepticism about the IRC to such an extent that they feared their future careers might be compromised by belonging to it. I had to resort to unusual sources. While visiting Israel a few months earlier as a member of a British trade delegation, I was so struck by the performance of a young Second Secretary at the Embassy in Tel Aviv that I offered him a job in my bank. He politely declined but it now occurred to me that he might feel differently about becoming chief of staff at the IRC. By chance an Air France flight taking me to Bangkok on business a few days later was scheduled to make a refuelling stop at Tel Aviv and I invited the young man in question, Roger Brooke, to meet me for a few minutes' chat at the airport. I asked whether he would join me if I persuaded the Foreign Office to second him for two or three years. After quick consultation with his wife he agreed and the Foreign Office proved agreeably accommodating over making him available.

All hell then broke loose in the rest of Whitehall. I was summoned by George Brown and asked if I had taken leave of my senses. He had taken his own life in his hands by appointing me, a mere merchant banker, to mastermind industrial re-organization; what would people think if my running mate in that task was to be an ex-Second Secretary of the British Embassy in Tel Aviv? I reminded Brown that I was to be allowed to appoint my staff unhindered. He grunted and said that he would have to consider the matter. He then telephoned each of my board members in turn to try to influence them against the appointment of Roger Brooke. And just to make sure that no stone was left unturned he engineered a telephone call to my home from a senior Treasury mandarin to warn me (most improperly, because it was quite untrue) that, even if I did the right thing in choosing a diplomat, Brooke was not the man since his own superiors did not think all that highly of him. Needless to say this judgement was utterly wrong. Not only did Brooke do a superb job at the IRC; he has since become an acclaimed leader in the private sector. The incident opened my eyes to one of the less endearing characteristics of the British civil service: their readiness to resort to tricks when thwarted.

Recruiting the remaining executives proved a less dramatic but still daunting task. I had to pursue very personal contacts – through my solicitor, my accountant and others – to find men of the quality and independence I needed. I found them in the end and take pride in the fact that within a few years all these men (I am ashamed to have to admit that there was not one woman among them) graduated to very high posts in British industry. It gave me a taste I never lost for steering bright young professionals towards congenial careers.

My instructions from the government were to waste no time and to act as though the appropriate legislation had already reached the statute book. I carefully refrained from doing anything of the kind but used the interval to sound out both industry and the City as to where they felt there might be a need for us. Not surprisingly, I encountered a mass of scepticism and in many quarters downright hostility. I spent my time giving personal assurances to industry that whatever powers Parliament ultimately gave us we would not use them to force mergers on unwilling parties. I was even more explicit *vis-à-vis* the banks and told them that I would seek unambiguous disclaimers from them in each case that our action was not considered an intrusion on their territory.

I think both industry and the City believed what I said; the trouble was that in the circumstances I was unlikely to survive for long. The kind of interventionist policy George Brown had in mind could only be orchestrated by an enthusiast who believed in the practicality of a planned economy and in the concept of Whitehall 'backing winners'. In the last resort one either subscribed to the notion that the man in Whitehall knew best or one did not. I had been recruited in the hope that I would somehow fudge this issue; the discovery that this was not my style dawned only slowly.

A unique distinction I enjoyed at that time was the possession of a secret numbered account at the Bank of England. The IRC was not yet a statutory body and had no claim on Treasury funding; yet we were already spending money on salaries, premises and research. George Brown asked me to have a word with the Governor of the Bank of England, the amiable Leslie O'Brien, to see what could be done. Suitably primed, O'Brien opened a Swiss-style numbered account for us on which I could draw up to £100,000.

The IRC Bill had a predictably rough passage in both Houses of Parliament but eventually received Royal Assent in December 1966. The informality of our constitution would have been unthinkable in any other country, least of all under a socialist administration. Not only was the spending of £150 million of public money in those days a very impressive sum, entrusted to a board consisting entirely of private individuals (who in turn left many of the decisions to a managing director who had expressed himself sceptically about the whole venture); more surprisingly still, there were almost no rules of engagement beyond a few general criteria (to which Lord Adlington wisely managed in the Lords debate to add 'corporate profitability') as to how the money was to be spent. Idle curiosity prompted me to ask my family lawyer, the late Lord Tangley, whether disbursing the whole £150 million to a consultant who claimed to know how to improve British industry and make it more profitable would be *ultra vires*; he said no but warned me against trying.

One evening I attended a dinner at the French Embassy for Georges Pompidou, then Prime Minister of France, who had come to London on a two-day official visit, accompanied by the Foreign Minister, Couve de Murville. The Ambassador sat me next to Pompidou after dinner and asked me to explain the IRC's constitution to him. Pompidou was stunned and made me repeat it to Couve. Their neat Cartesian minds were visibly outraged by such informality!

Another aspect of British informality – which Americans would have found incomprehensible – was how difficult I found it to persuade the Whitehall mandarins to accept that I had placed my family's shareholdings in the care of trustees. It seemed a prudent thing to do, given the controversy likely to develop over some of the IRC's activities; yet the IRC Act did not provide for it and the mandarins were embarrassed by my action: 'nobody else was doing it', they said. Fortunately the only two quarters from which any of my actions were even mildly impugned on conflict of interest grounds were *The Times* and the late Sir Jules Thorn. Both talked or wrote rubbish and no one took a blind bit of notice of what they said. When I went to Brussels six years later as an international civil servant, I had even greater difficulty persuading the European Commission to take notice of my private trust arrangements; clearly this form of due diligence had still not crossed the Atlantic.

Just as the IRC was getting into its stride, the Board received an invitation from Harold Wilson to dine with him and other Cabinet colleagues at Downing Street on 5 November 1966. We were told that it was a working dinner; the Prime Minister wanted to hear our views on the IRC's likely role in the current economic climate. My wife and I were to be on our honeymoon in America that week. We reluctantly agreed to cut this short and returned to London.

There was much tension at the time between business and government and the Confederation of British Industry had recently issued a statement severely criticising the government's handling of the economy and pouring scorn on the IRC initiative. Both my chairman Frank Kearton and I felt that there was a risk that anything of an even mildly upbeat nature which we might say at the Wilson dinner could be used by government spokesmen as evidence that there existed 'another' group of industrialists less hostile to the administration than the CBI. We therefore agreed to meet and settle on a common line at Brooks's Club an hour or so before the dinner. No sooner had I explained its purpose than Sir Frank Schon, an IRC director and close friend of Wilson's, voiced his dismay that it should even have entered our heads that such a guileless fellow as the Prime Minister could have had anything other than sheer conviviality in mind when he invited us and that we should feel thoroughly ashamed of ourselves for having attributed other motives to him. It was this sort of crass innocence which was to give me more trouble at the IRC than interference from government.

6

Tinkering with Industry

THE SEMI OFFICIAL HISTORY of the IRC, written many years later, has this to say of me: 'Without Grierson, the IRC would not have been what it was. Equally, until he left it, the Corporation was not likely to become what it did.' My departure, it claims, 'removed a powerful influence for caution', and I would not quarrel with this view. My foot was almost permanently on the brake, trying to abort projects which were either patently unwise or which the market could perform better. Our first real challenge – and one we could have done without – came in December 1966 in the shape of an acute financial crisis at Rootes, the car company in which Chrysler had taken a 40 per cent interest.

Fate had already cast me for a walk-on part in an earlier instalment of that saga. In 1963 the then Lord Rootes announced proudly – somewhat too proudly – that Chrysler had acquired a minority interest in his family business and had undertaken not to seek a majority. In praising this in the House of Commons, Reggie Maudling, then Chancellor of the

Exchequer, congratulated Rootes somewhat fulsomely on this singular mark of American confidence in the way the business was run. Next morning, as Chrysler's financial adviser in London, I received a call from Detroit expressing surprise at the Chancellor's remarks since Rootes had in writing agreed to let Chrysler raise their stake to a majority should they later find it expedient to do so. I was asked to seek an early meeting with the Chancellor to clarify this explosive issue. He received me that very afternoon at 11 Downing Street.

Maudling was flanked by one of the great Establishment wizards of the 1960s, the late Sir William Armstrong. Both immediately understood the gravity of the matter: the Chancellor had inadvertently misled the House of Commons. Maudling instructed Armstrong to find a solution and the following day I was treated to one of those truly spectacular performances of mandarin brilliance to which the Treasury rises on such occasions. In the Chancellor's presence, this time in his Treasury office, Armstrong waved his magic wand: a planted question was to be asked in the House of Commons demanding details of the Chrysler deal to which the Chancellor would reply (this having meanwhile been cleared with Detroit) that Chrysler 'would not *over the objections of the British government of the day* increase its holding above 50 per cent'. A veritable masterpiece of ambiguity which got everybody off the hook.

Little did I suspect that three years later, wearing an entirely different hat, I would be called upon to untangle this elegant ambiguity. Heather and I had just set out on our second attempt at a honeymoon. On returning to our Austrian hotel from a day's skiing I found an urgent message to telephone Anthony Wedgwood Benn, then Minister of Technology. I did so and was told that an acute crisis had developed at Rootes: the company had run out of cash and credit and was unable to meet bills maturing in less than a week. £20 million were urgently needed which Chrysler were ready to inject against an increase in their shareholding to about 60 per cent. The government was extremely reluctant to sanction this and the Maudling–Armstrong formula of 1963 gave them the power to stop it.

In an attempt to find a 'British solution', a favourite phrase of the interventionist state, Benn had summoned Sir George Harriman of the British Motor Corporation and Sir Donald Stokes of Leyland, then the two leading British car magnates, to his London home the following afternoon – a Sunday – and Benn wondered if I would join the party and help him persuade Harriman and Stokes to do something they were likely to approach with great reluctance. I told Benn that my immediate sympathy lay with Harriman and Stokes: why was the government so fussed about Chrysler performing the rescue and controlling what was only the third largest British car company? Benn assured me that this was a matter of the utmost importance to the Cabinet and that he would appreciate my coming back to see what I could do.

I was not best pleased at the prospect of the IRC becoming even marginally involved in this unnecessary manoeuvre, not to mention yet another interrupted honeymoon. But I decided to return and was whisked straight from London airport to Benn's house in Holland Park Road where Harriman and Stokes had already consumed innumerable mugs of Benn's tea. It took them and me little time to agree that there was absolutely no case for either British Motors or Leyland pouring £20 million into an ailing Rootes and that no public interest would be threatened by allowing Chrysler to do the bail-out.

An unhappy Benn tried to talk me into letting the IRC perform the rescue alone. I said that I would resign rather than lend my hand to that. Sensing that he was getting nowhere, Benn rang Jim Callaghan, the Chancellor, who agreed to see us at once. We proceeded to Downing Street and were ushered into Callaghan's study. The only other person in the room was

Peter Jay, his son-in-law and private secretary, who took notes recording our conversation with scrupulous fairness. Callaghan was his usual charming self and added his own eloquent pleas for a British solution to Benn's earlier efforts. He fared no better and everyone agreed that the Prime Minister would now have to take a decision.

Word reached me the following day that the Cabinet saw the strength of my reasoning but could not see their way to 'handing over' the company to Chrysler. Could I devise some face-saving formula? My staff and I went to work and by evening we had devised a cosmetic artefact enabling the government to let Chrysler take control without undue loss of face. Unfortunately, from our point of view, it involved a nominal role for the IRC; and, while this seemed a worthwhile price to pay for letting the market do its thing, I suspected – correctly, as it turned out – that the press would present it in such a way as to rob us at a stroke of the entire public relations ground we had laboriously gained in the past six months. In fact the IRC's role was minimal and entirely cosmetic. We were to provide £5 million of the £20 million needed under the unconditional guarantee of Chrysler and to put one director (not even an IRC member) on the Rootes Board. Our willingness to perform this risk-free charade enabled Benn to announce to the House the following afternoon that the IRC had saved Rootes for Britain by making it possible for the government to allow Chrysler to bail it out.

To pad his announcement, Benn insisted on obtaining commitments from Chrysler about the way they would run Rootes. None of these commitments had real value, but for more than two hours that evening I shuttled between the Prime Minister's room in the Commons and a committee room downstairs where the high command of Chrysler and Rootes and their respective bankers sat awaiting their fate. The Prime Minister personally drafted a large part of the document to which Chrysler were required to put their name and my job was to get this agreed – a task calling for much redrafting – without the two sides actually meeting. Feydeau could not have improved on the absurdity of this farce.

The press treatment of the IRC role in this rescue was as disastrous as I had feared. The government's opponents seized on it as a foretaste of what they most dreaded. In my frustration I went to see the new Lord Rootes (his father having died) to ask him whether he would make a statement that what the IRC had done was precisely what Rootes had asked for. He pretended not to know what I was talking about and all but threw me out of his office. It was a revealing experience at the hands of an industrial grandee.

In the months that followed my staff and I studied a number of situations which appeared to offer scope for IRC assistance. Some of these came from government departments and nationalized industries; others were brought to us by companies or their bankers; still others were the product of our own thinking. Very few passed the stringent tests we imposed on ourselves; one of the exceptions was a loan of £15 million to the English Electric Corporation to induce the company to absorb another large electronics concern, Eliott Automation, which was finding it difficult to exist on its own and whose survival was deemed important for national security.

In addition, several attempts were made by Whitehall to interest me in the idea of a merger between British Motors and Leyland. My soundings made me sceptical about the prospect of what could only be a shotgun marriage with the Leyland finger on the trigger. My unwillingness to force this project through caused great disappointment in government circles and was one of the factors which persuaded Wedgwood Benn that he must have a new instrument of his own – eventually to emerge as the Industry Act of 1968 – to do what the IRC would not do. British Motors and Leyland were finally brought to the altar by my successor with results that are now part of history.

A recollection of my IRC days which still makes me chuckle was a conference in London with the Keidanren, Japan's industrial federation. Leaders of the CBI had been in Japan the previous year and the Japanese were paying their return visit. The CBI Chairman, John Partridge of Imperial Tobacco, extended a special invitation to me to help him reassure our Japanese friends about the harmlessness of the IRC. On the second day the President of the Keidanren rose to ask a question – through an interpreter – about the nature of the IRC and managed to make it clear that the Japanese had a pretty low opinion of it. John Partridge proceeded calmly to refute everything the Japanese had alleged; and when the Keidanren President rose a second time to reiterate some of his poisonous remarks, he asked him from whom he had obtained his obviously slanted information. 'From Sir Duncan Oppenheim at dinner in San Francisco last month' came the instant reply. Sir Duncan, then Chairman of the British–American Tobacco Company, was at the table and looked highly embarrassed. I absolutely loved it and begged for the exchange to go verbatim into the record.

Another memorable event was a one-day conference chaired by Harold Wilson at Lancaster House to discuss the problems of British industry. We sat in three phalanxes – industry, unions and government – trotting out many hoary old myths about big being beautiful, winners needing to be picked and the alleged role of German banks in making German industry efficient. But what made this conference hard to forget was Harold Wilson's systematic rubbishing of all service industries as 'candyfloss'. British socialists could not bring themselves in those days to look on any industry not served by the big unions (and casting block votes at TUC conferences) as a reliable source of lasting employment; it was a mistake corrected – perhaps over-corrected – only under Margaret Thatcher.

One of our more innocent remits at the IRC was to help exporters. We set about this in unconventional ways. At one point we were alerted to the fact that by way of retaliation for the British government's generally unfriendly attitude, Portugal had excluded British contractors from tendering for a very important power project in its African colonies. We were consulted as to what could be done. I asked Lord Cromer, who had recently retired from the Governorship of the Bank of England and was back at Baring Brothers, if he knew of anything the Portuguese authorities wanted from Britain. It took him no time to discover that the Portuguese Telephone Company had a technical problem with our Treasury over sterling borrowings which they were anxious to resolve. We persuaded the Chancellor of the Exchequer to rule on it in Portugal's favour. This enabled us to ask Cromer to go to Lisbon, a capital not much visited by senior UK officials or businessmen at that time, and through a judiciously timed announcement of the Treasury concession to obtain the inclusion of UK tenderers in the African project. Using an invitation to address the UK Chamber of Commerce in Lisbon as pretext, Cromer agreed; but he rightly insisted on first obtaining from George Brown, by then Foreign Secretary, an assurance that he would refrain from saying rude things about Portugal for the duration of his stay in Lisbon. Cromer and I called on Brown at the Foreign Office. His solemn promise to be good about Portugal for five whole days is an enjoyable memory.

In 1967 in the middle of my IRC service, I received a summons from Herbert Bowden, the Lord President of the Council, to serve as Lord Robens's deputy on a mission the government had agreed to send to Malta. The Maltese Prime Minister had been jumping up and down in London to express the islanders' dismay at the recently announced withdrawal of British forces and our mission was to assess the prospects of Malta's economic survival after their departure.

We spent ten agreeable days in Valletta listening to everybody who wanted to give evidence; and we came to the comforting conclusion – published in an official report – that life in Malta was possible after the British servicemen had gone. On our return to London, Robens and I went to see Jim Callaghan, the Chancellor, in his room at the Commons to report on certain delicate aspects of the future of the Malta docks. As we left, Callaghan casually asked Robens how things were going in the coal industry of which he was Chairman. 'Fine,' said Robens, 'we've just closed two more uneconomic pits and are about to shut down a third.'

'Good', said Callaghan, then asked cautiously where the third was. On learning that it was in his constituency, his tone changed. I was politely made aware that my presence was no longer required – and clearly missed a lot of fun!

Another adventure I recall with nostalgia was an encounter with George Brown in New York. He had just become Foreign Secretary. We bumped into each other in the lobby of the Carlyle Hotel in New York. Clearly forgetting that I was no longer part of his bailiwick, he swept me into the lift and up to his penthouse suite where the Israeli Foreign Minister, Abba Eban, and a large Israeli delegation were waiting to see him. Before I could remind Brown that my remit was industry not foreign affairs, I found myself sitting with the British delegation opposite Eban and his colleagues. Brown had to be heavily nudged by senior officials before I was allowed to leave the meeting.

At about this time my Chairman, Frank Kearton, for whom in other respects I had great admiration and even a good deal of affection, chose in a programme on Granada TV to make the extraordinary assertion – of which he had given me no warning – that the IRC honeymoon with industry and the City was over and that 'now the boot goes in'. It can be imagined what effect this had on our relations with industry which had barely recovered from the aftermath of the Rootes affair; I went to see Michael Stewart (who had exchanged roles with George Brown and was now our Minister) and asked him to find a successor for my post who shared Kearton's views. The government took no notice of this and I had to remind Stewart several times in the coming months. Meanwhile I soldiered on.

My swansong was the merger of GEC and AEI, a transaction about which several books have been written and which is frequently cited as justification for the existence of the IRC. It was in fact nothing of the kind. What gave the shrewd heads at GEC the correct impression that their bid for AEI would find favour in official circles was not the existence of the IRC but the prevalence in Whitehall of a mood of which the IRC was itself an expression and which could be relied upon to sanction the merger. GEC also knew better than most how to play on the vanity and self-importance of such a body.

It was this issue which provoked my resignation. My colleagues, in a mood of high excitement, were prepared to back Weinstock against any other solution of the problem of AEI's impending doom. I on the other hand took the view that a statutory body using taxpayers' money had no right to depart from a position of strict neutrality if more than one way of solving the problem presented itself. I was not prepared to compromise on this and resigned. Peter Shore, then Secretary of State for Economic Affairs, wrote me a charming letter – released to the press – thanking me generously on the government's behalf for my services. It was an elegant gesture, given the troublesome time the Labour government had had with me.

7

Afterthoughts

TO MY GREAT ASTONISHMENT, my resignation earned me half the
front page of *The Times* the following morning. In a public
context it was of course supremely unimportant. The government's industrial policy, stated by *The Times* to be endangered
by my departure, survived effortlessly; and an enthusiast was
found to take my place.

I had learned some useful lessons, not least that when one
resigns from public office on a point of principle it is best to say
so plainly rather than consent to some mealy-mouthed formula
about leaving 'to pursue other interests'. I was inexperienced in
that domain and had no wish to make GEC's task more
difficult. However, the press treated me well. I also made the
discovery that the number of letters one receives on leaving an
official post is about one-tenth of those one gets on being
appointed.

My IRC service clearly revealed to me the pitfalls of state
intervention in industry masquerading as industrial policy.
Discussion of this topic tends to be overlaid with semantic

confusion. What is at issue is not the right of government to use fiscal, monetary, procurement and other levers to nudge industry in directions which it judges beneficial; few nowadays dispute this. Nor is there much argument about the occasional duty of government to descend into the economic arena and deal with an industrial emergency when it arises. These are legitimate exercises of sovereignty for which governments are held accountable at the next election. By contrast, the pursuit by a semi governmental body like the IRC of a capricious policy of random intervention is a highly questionable proposition for which it is hard to find justification. Neither its achievements nor its failures can ever be more than a drop in the ocean compared with the consequences of other public policies. A single error of judgement by the Chancellor of the Exchequer in the realm of fiscal policy would easily outweigh the whole *oeuvre* of an IRC. Moreover, the existence of this kind of twilight body tends to create artificial and sinister distinctions between 'good' and 'bad' industrialists, those who make themselves agreeable to the authorities and those who prefer to go about their business on their own. Unfortunately, the most valuable contributions to economic progress do not always come from the former.

Another pitfall of which we quickly became aware was that by its very nature the IRC came to be looked upon as a source of 'blessings' for industrial restructuring. The IRC's approval could turn a lame-duck situation into a 'rationalization' of national importance; more useful still it could protect a merger from the rigour of competition law. Another spurious value attributed to the IRC was that it could 'handle' industrial problems more effectively than ministers or civil servants. I never understood why a small group of quite ordinary human beings, seconded temporarily from their normal work, should be presumed to possess wisdom and judgement on that scale. The implied insult to our civil servants seemed to me wholly

At school in Paris, Lycée Pasteur,
1933 (fourth from right, second
row)

Platoon Commander in North
Africa, 1943

Honouring the French Resistance at a ceremony in Brittany, 1948

At ECE plenary meeting in Geneva, 1947. Sitting next to Executive Secretary, Professor Gunnar Myrdal

A well-known scene at London airport in 1956 whose photographic record was never actually been seen: two guardians of the law gently persuading one very late passenger that sitting under the aircraft's wing would not succeed in getting the doors re-opened for him to board his Paris flight!

En route to Moscow with Roy Thomson in an 8-engined Tupolev, 1961

In Washington, 1958, with the Peruvian Ambassador and the Vice-President of the World Bank witnessing the signature of a loan to the Peruvian Railways

On the footplate, 16,000 feet above sea-level, in the Peruvian Andes: with colleague Eric Korner, 1961

Newly married, 1968, on mission to Singapore, with Prime Minister and Mrs Lee

A year later – at the christening of son Jacob

The IRC's first board meeting with George Brown in attendance – and Sam Courtauld looking down critically from the wall! (*The Times*)

Inauguration of the new Brussels Headquarters of the European Organisation for Cancer Treatment Research: the author with the Duke of Edinburgh, President of the Organisation

In New York with Chrysler
Chairman, Lee Iacocca, and
the President of Fiat, Gianni
Agnelli, 1988

For ten years (1977–87) the
author was co-owner of a
peanut farm in Georgia – and
a major customer of the Bell
Telephone Company!

Her Majesty The Queen switching on the Christmas decorations
at the Royal Festival Hall

Escorting HRH The Princess Royal to a Reception in the Hayward Gallery to mark th
first anniversary of the South Bank Centre

undeserved; and when I was later interviewed by the Fulton Commission on the Civil Service I said so. The manner in which civil servants and ministers handled the Cunard Company crisis in 1967, to quote just one example, seemed to me every bit as skilful as anything the IRC could have achieved in similar circumstances.

Finally, it would be unwise to ignore the fact that the mere existence of a safety-net like the IRC tempts businessmen to undertake more high-wire work than is good for them. The danger of an organization created for the specific purpose of helping those who cannot help themselves is that it tends to reduce the responsibility they take for their actions. Far better to let those in trouble find their own way to the appropriate department in Whitehall and struggle to get a hearing.

The kindest verdict on the IRC is that it was a psychiatrist's couch for businessmen to unburden themselves informally of their problems while at the same time permitting IRC officials to take the initiative in chatting them up on what they suspected these problems to be. But this rests on the flawed assumption that there is a natural convergence between the interests of government and those of business which only short-sightedness or lack of understanding fail to achieve. Terms such as 'mixed economy' and 'consensus' are symptomatic of this belief. But in real life the prime duty of government is to protect its citizens from abuse of economic power; and a policy too obsessively concerned with the interests of producers cannot achieve this. What is needed is a tough stance in support of a carefully thought out position, not vague chasing after consensus.

Just how differently enthusiasts for the corporate state judge these matters is evident from the verdict of Professor Grigor McClelland, an erstwhile IRC board member and later Director of the Manchester Business School. Assessing the IRC in 1972, he wrote: 'The IRC was perhaps the most novel, most high-powered, most entrepreneurial, most publicized, most controversial, but ultimately the most significant and successful, of the innovations in economic management introduced by the Labour government of 1964–70.' What a lot this tells you about the other 'innovations'!

Although the IRC was not my happiest experience, I must in fairness say that Labour ministers, including the redoubtable Mr Benn, behaved impeccably even when I rejected their pet schemes; at no time did they seek to put pressure on me to change my mind. If Wilson or other senior ministers were irritated by the abruptness of my resignation, they never showed it and Wilson in particular treated me with great courtesy on all subsequent occasions. What did slightly embarrass me, however, was the discovery – again made in Brussels five years later – of how easy it is to have one's way in public life if one is prepared to make a noisy fuss. The Establishment pays a high price for a quiet time. Taking advantage of this does not make one popular but is remarkably effective. (Just how unpopular it made me was revealed to me years later by Harold Lever from whom I learnt, not wholly to my surprise, that I was easily Whitehall's least favourite dollar-a-year man!)

My stormiest relationship was inevitably with George Brown himself. He was a bully and one had to stand up to him. But there were moments when one grew quite fond of the old boy and his attitude to the IRC was nothing if not robust and practical. The first time I called on him he had just returned from a high-level meeting with French ministers. He made me aware of his no-nonsense approach by commenting plaintively that, whereas he and Wilson had copiously flagged briefing books in front of them, their French opposite numbers appeared to rely entirely on their memories.

Almost the last time I saw him was when as Foreign Secretary he dined at our house the night of the so-called

D-Notice affair. In the middle of dinner he was called to the telephone to be told that a story about the security services was being printed that night by the *Daily Express* in defiance of a D-Notice. Brown telephoned the Chairman of the *Express* at the London Club where he was dining and got the impression (wrongly as it turned out) that he had persuaded him to stop the story; that anyhow is what he told us when he re-appeared smiling in the dining-room twenty minutes later. The security story did appear next morning and the subsequent inquiry by a Committee of Privy Councillors turned partly on whether Brown was entitled to assume that he had succeeded in stopping it. Brown did not handle his side very skilfully and to this day I do not understand why no one summoned me as a witness; I could at least have testified that Brown at that moment was convinced that he had stopped publication.

8

More Truancy

HAVING TAKEN MY LEAVE of the IRC I returned to my desk at the
bank and accepted an invitation from Arnold Weinstock to
become Vice-Chairman of GEC. I had clearly been forgiven for
endangering the AEI bid. I also joined one or two other boards
and became Chairman of the Orion Bank, an international
affiliate of National Westminster.

My earlier pattern of temporary involvement in public
affairs soon reasserted itself. But in June 1968 I astonished
myself by actually turning down the offer of a public job.
Christopher Soames had been appointed Ambassador to Paris
and I was invited by the Minister of State at the Foreign Office,
Alun Chalfont, to go to Paris with Soames as a supernumary
minister for trade and industrial matters. I was sorely tempted
to accept but felt that, having just become Vice-Chairman of
GEC, I could not chuck that job and disappear to Paris. I
regretted my decision afterwards.

Almost immediately after I had taken up my GEC duties I
was asked to lead a special mission to Singapore. The

circumstances were extraordinarily reminiscent of Malta to the point where I began to suspect that my name must have got on some Whitehall list of citizens with experience of former colonies about to lose their military garrisons. As in Malta, but on a much bigger scale, notice had been served on Singapore that its large contingent of British servicemen, spending about £300 million a year, would shortly be withdrawn. With little else to support the economy, Singapore's tough-minded, charismatic Prime Minister, Harry Lee, had come to London to plead his country's plight with the British government. What could Britain do to help Singapore convert the massive military installations to productive industrial use? It was a question to which there was no easy answer. Following the time-honoured practice of establishing a committee when stuck for an answer, the government urgently requested the CBI – in the middle of the 1968 summer holidays – to send a mission to Singapore to study Singapore's economic problem and make recommendations on what use could be made of the military installations to promote industry. I was invited to lead this mission.

After extensive briefings at the Ministry of Defence we set out for Singapore on 13 August, my wife accompanying me. For seven days we 'explored' in depth every army barracks, navy depot and RAF station, and as we emerged from each the entire Singapore TV and press lay in wait to cross-examine us on our conclusions. Into what kind of factory did we think one could transform this naval depot or that RAF hangar – textiles, electronics or shoes? We gave evasive answers, reserving our overall conclusions for a press conference scheduled for the last day of our stay.

I had several private meetings with Prime Minister Lee and developed enormous admiration for the way he handled the situation. No one could at that time have remotely foreseen the stunning economic success which the industrious people of Singapore and their enlightened rulers would within a few years snatch from the jaws of disaster. Our final communiqué struck a guardedly upbeat note and we delivered ourselves of a number of optimistic generalizations about the use of military installations; yet what subsequently happened made our observations look feeble. (One thing which irritated us during this mission and to which I insisted on referring in our communiqué was that at the very moment when we were discussing ways and means of increasing British investment in Singapore, 10 Downing Street was sounding off about the wickedness of the City of London making investments abroad instead of backing Britain.)

So tense was the relationship between Singapore and neighbouring Malaysia that when the Malaysian government heard of our trip they put strong diplomatic pressure on the Foreign Office to make us stop off in Kuala Lumpur on our way home. Though there was no obvious reason to do so we complied with the request and after finishing our business in Singapore flew to Kuala Lumpur where our brief was to investigate how British investment in general could be increased. But on the second day of our Malaysian visit I received a telegram that the Plessey Company were bidding for English Electric. Sensing that this was a situation GEC would not let go unchallenged, I asked my deputy to take charge of the mission, apologised to the government of Malaysia and flew home to what turned out to be a fierce and fascinating battle.

Though ultimately successful – Plessey having to accept defeat and English Electric becoming part of GEC – the episode had a tailpiece which made me brutally aware of the frailty of human sentiment in business. The Warburg merchant bank, of which I was still a director, saw nothing wrong in complying with an ultimatum from Plessey, whom they represented, for my immediate resignation from their board because of my GEC connection, even though this brought to an end an association of more than twenty years. I look back on it as one of the shabbier experiences of my business life.

Among my extracurricular activities at that time was an invitation from Keith Joseph to sit on a Tory party committee making preparations for government. It was my first direct exposure to party politics and I thoroughly enjoyed it. It also, I hope, gave some pleasure to Sir Frank Schon, my former IRC colleague, who at last felt confirmed in the suspicion which he used to voice freely (but alas without foundation) that my reluctance to let the IRC do a bit of bullying had something to do with wishing to please my Tory friends.

My IRC past pursued me in small ways during those years. In 1970 I was alerted to the fact that my successor had authorized the writing of an offical history of the IRC and had been granted access to confidential IRC files. Since I had given the industrialists and bankers with whom I dealt a solemn undertaking that their conversations with us were off the record (the basis of our work demanded no less) I was appalled to hear that such an indiscretion was contemplated, at any rate so soon after the event, and my intervention in Whitehall succeeded in postponing the project by some ten years and reducing the indiscretions of the book. A senior British civil servant, Antony Part, taught me a lesson in humility in connection with this episode. I had been to see him with my complaint. Unable to obtain sympathy, I voiced my disappointment in a rather strongly worded letter. In reply he quoted Benjamin Franklin:

> We must not in the Course of Publick Life expect immediate Approbation and immediate grateful Acknowledgement of our Services. But let us persevere thro' Abuse and even Injury. The internal Satisfaction of a good Conscience is always present, and Time will do us justice in the Minds of the People, even of those at present the most prejudic'd against us.

I got the point.

In 1971 I received an invitation from the French Minister of

Industry, André Bettencourt, to dine with him at his house in Neuilly. President Pompidou had asked him, possibly recalling our conversation at the French Embassy five years earlier, to consult me on his government's project of launching an IRC-type operation in France. I tried to be factual but could not avoid revealing my bias. I need not have worried because Pompidou's mind was evidently made up in advance and the French IDI (Institut de Développement Industriel) soon appeared on the scene. It was a less pretentious creature than our IRC and its successes and failures were equally insignificant in the national context.

Finally 1971 saw the decision by the Heath government to abolish the IRC. All of a sudden this erstwhile *bête noire* acquired well-wishers in the business community – those who had benefited from its largesse as well as those still hoping for handouts – and there were pleas for its retention from the most unlikely quarters. It was a far cry from 1966 and showed that the corporate state has its devotees even in the sacred heartland of private enterprise.

Another year was to go by before my next spell of full-time public service. Meanwhile, the birth of our son Jacob in May 1969 dominated our lives. He has enriched our existence ever since and is now an undergraduate at Oxford.

9

Bureaucrat in Brussels

MY BRUSSELS ASSIGNMENT dropped out of the clear blue sky. European integration had always been close to my heart and I regretted Britain's coolness towards it. But I had never been a Euro-fanatic nor belonged to any of the pressure groups lobbying for British entry.

I was having breakfast with my wife one November morning in 1972 when the telephone rang and the unmistakable voice of my old friend Christopher Soames, who had recently been named Vice-President of the Brussels Commission, came on the line. Would I help the government on a small problem which had arisen?

I enquired what the problem was. Britain had been offered the important-sounding post of Director-General for Industry and the Prime Minister was anxious that we should fill it. There was however a difficulty. The eminent but eccentric Italian Communist, Altiero Spinelli, then Commissioner for Industry, had fielded his own protégé for the post – a British economist whom he had somewhat oddly recruited to his staff long before

British entry – and HMG had profound reservations about this. The only way out of the dilemma was for Britain to field a rival candidate with a strong industrial background. Would I drop everything and oblige for a couple of years?

My first reaction was not enthusiastic. I would have to go to Brussels almost at once and did not see how I could abandon my various colleagues at such short notice. Moreover, the prospect of heading a large bureaucracy bent on *dirigiste* adventures, when I had only recently escaped from a similar fate in Britain, was distinctly chilling. But Soames was a man to whom it was difficult to say no. Besides, the idea of working with him for a couple of years in the heady atmosphere of an enlarged Community was not wholly unattractive. In any case Brussels was a city I knew well – having lived there briefly in the early 50s – and our three-year-old son was of an age when he could be transplanted without fuss. I told Soames that I wanted to meet Spinelli before making up my mind.

Arrangements were made for the two of us to dine in a Brussels restaurant the following week. I could not help being immediately fascinated by the charm and erudition of this veteran of the Italian Left whom Mussolini had jailed for almost sixteen years, some of them on the grim prison island of Ventotene, a kind of Mediterranean Alcatraz. I sensed that working with him would be a challenge, but I also realized that as in the IRC my hand would constantly be reaching for the brakes. To misquote Churchill on de Gaulle, Spinelli seemed a man with both feet planted firmly on the clouds!

My friends were divided in their advice. I was fifty-one years old; even if I stayed in Brussels for only two years, my career would have suffered too many interruptions to be easily resumed. I decided nevertheless to take the plunge. Almost the only condition I stipulated was that Soames should personally write to the Chairman of the National Westminster Bank over whose affiliate I presided and explain that the responsibility for my hasty departure – I succeeded in delaying it until April 1973 – lay wholly with the government. He did so in a letter of great charm and I managed to persuade my old friend and colleague, Harold Caccia, fifteen years my senior, to take my place at the bank until a long-term successor could be found.

Ted Heath was gracious about my taking the job. He wrote me a letter thanking me for 'allowing my arm to be twisted' and invited Heather and me to lunch at Chequers to meet Jean Monnet, the Community's founding father. He also asked me to No. 10 for a general talk about the Community a few days before I left to take up my assignment. A somewhat colder douche was administered by John Hunt, the senior civil servant dealing with European affairs in the Cabinet office. He came to lunch with me and read from the brief his staff had prepared. After a while, he arrived at the sensible conclusion that it would be easier to let me read his brief. I still have it in my files; its unambiguous message was: 'Tell Grierson that the less he does in Brussels the better'!

My journey to Brussels proceeded somewhat unconventionally by way of Peking. The previous summer I had received an invitation from the Bank of China to visit China as the Bank's guest. My wife and stepdaughter were included in the invitation. China was not at the time organized for tourism and this kind of invitation, especially from the Bank of China, which enjoyed special status in the bureaucracy, was a rare privilege. We accepted to go in Easter 1973, but my subsequent appointment to a senior international post clearly raised a problem. The Chinese had invited me as a banker; I was now a civil servant. Moreover, the organization I served had no diplomatic relations with China. I put the dilemma to Soames who consulted the Commission. No one seemed to want to take a decision and I was only told what was expected of me in late March, two weeks before my departure. My instructions were to advise my Chinese hosts forthwith of my changed status; if, as anticipated, they still wanted me to go, I was to conduct myself as a banker but also to try to find out what the Chinese attitude to the Community was and whether they seriously wished to have relations with it.

This turned out to be no problem at all. The Chinese authorities were fascinated by what was going on in Brussels. They had no contact with the Community and were anxious to establish relations. Conversation in each Chinese city began on banking topics but quickly strayed to questions about the Community's constitution and in particular whether the Treaty of Rome provided for missions from non-member states. I answered these questions as best I could, conscious that I was the first Community official to visit China. Soon after my return diplomatic feelers were put out from Brussels. These eventually led to Christopher Soames visiting Peking and to diplomatic relations being established.

My debut in Brussels as chief of Directorate-General III, the Department of Industry, proved a sad case of crossed signals. The fact that I had been head of Britain's IRC was wrongly taken by my new colleagues as evidence that they were being joined by a committed interventionist ready to support moves towards a planned European economy. In their defence it has to be said that the loose wording of official communiqués at the time of British entry fostered this kind of misunderstanding. Talk about the need to establish 'a single industrial base', apart from being meaningless, could easily be interpreted as a clarion call for a command economy.

A key difficulty in Brussels in 1973 (which I believe persists to this day) was that a Director-General, though a grandee in the bureaucracy, had no real control over his staff. With much lobbying – and some help from Whitehall – I was allowed to form a small private office to which I recruited two bright young men, Ruy Brandolini, a nephew of Gianni Agnelli, and Roger Lewis, the son of one of my GEC colleagues. The rest of my staff, some 150, owed their positions to an established but unattractive process of intergovernmental horsetrading which ensured that there could be no sacking or demotion; it also deprived the Director-General, their nominal chief, of any real influence over what they did. Thus my senior subordinates – and a few junior ones too – regarded themselves as life tenants of feudal domains belonging by tradition to their nationality – Dutch for shipbuilding, UK for high technology, Italian for steel – which entitled them to produce 'policies' for their sectors without the slightest attempt to ascertain in advance whether even the Commission, let alone the governments, were willing to endorse them.

This had the disturbing effect of causing draft directives to arrive on my desk without my having had the remotest inkling of an intention to produce them. To those of us accustomed to more orderly legislative processes, where decisions are taken at the political level and only the drafting is done by officials, this came as something of a shock. And the shock was compounded when I discovered that, though their superiors were kept in ignorance, the authors of these 'from-the-hip' directives felt free to discuss them with their own governments and to leak them – virtually give them – to the press. Indiscretion was regarded as part of the evangelical duty of the Commission.

The founding fathers in their wisdom – and there was something to be said for it at the time – gave the Commission an unusual status: not quite an embryo government and yet more powerful than an international secretariat. To the outside world the Commission was the equal of the Council of Ministers; and it possessed the exclusive right to propose legislation. The trouble was that the Council retained the equally exclusive and more critical right to make decisions. The need to prove itself the Council's equal in the face of this difference gave the Commission a built-in inferiority complex for which it endeavoured from the start to compensate by an unending stream of initiatives. The fact that few of these passed the scrutiny of the Council and most were lost in a legislative cemetery did not greatly bother the Commission; their duty was discharged so long as they dangled alluring projects before the public.

I was reduced, as previously at the IRC, to running my blue pencil through a great deal of the paper that came across my desk. For someone dedicated to the cause of European cooperation, this was not an agreeable way of spending one's time; it was also quite ineffective since my staff knew how to bypass my veto and go straight to Commissioner Spinelli. My deputy, a charming Dutchman who had grown up in the service of the Commission, made no bones about it in a note he sent me: 'We should not be so concerned with the substance and presentation of our documents, but should rather get out as many as possible quickly without worrying too much about their contents.'

'Industrial policy' was an expression much bandied about in those heady days. The big European canvas presented attractive opportunities for *dirigiste* adventures beyond national boundaries; 'Brussels knows best' sounded as convincing as its Whitehall namesake. By contrast, the drudgery of removing one by one the remaining obstacles to free trade seemed desperately prosaic. My attempts to have it accepted in 1973 proved futile, but it has now, in its '1992' wrapping, become the dogma of the Commission.

An absurd amount of time was spent by my officials on two favourite pastimes: harmonization of company law, arguably one of the most futile exercises ever undertaken; and the promotion of high technology, a megalomaniac attempt to emulate on a European scale some very questionable spending by national governments. The trouble was that in those days only two departments in Brussels had real clout: agriculture and competition; both had acquired slices of sovereignty from national governments and agriculture had money as well. This created feelings of deep jealousy in other departments, notably my own; and it would be no exaggeration to say – and the feeling was often voiced openly at meetings – that policy proposals emanating from my staff were as a rule more concerned with keeping up with the Joneses in other departments than with the substance of the issues at stake.

One of my more embarrassing duties in Brussels was to have to listen to special pleading by delegations representing sectors of industry. Behind a barrage of flattery which made one wince – how easy it is to play on the self-importance of public officials – I was told what a fantastic opportunity lay before me of creating 'just the right environment' for this or that industry; invariably the right environment meant either protection or subsidy or both. One could not help recalling the famous dictum of President Coolidge: 'Nine-tenths of the President's callers come to ask for something they ought not to have.'

10

Exit from Brussels

BY THE END OF 1973 it became clear that my stay in Brussels was unlikely to last much longer. I made no secret of my frustrations to Christopher Soames and, while obviously hoping that I would stay as long as possible, he showed sympathy for my predicament.

Contrary to what many of my friends in Britain inferred from the newspapers, my problem with my Communist Commissioner was not his Communism, which hardly surfaced in our relationship, but his fanatical federalist convictions which led to an uncompromising refusal to deal with obstacles in a rational way. Like all federalists, Spinelli had great faith in the ability of public opinion, once aroused by the charms of federal Europe, to sound trumpets which would induce governments to abdicate in favour of Brussels. Much of his time was spent encouraging the design of super-blueprints to dazzle the media, even though he must have known that they stood no chance in the real world.

This led to some curious exchanges. One day we were

discussing European shipbuilding, where the existence of excess capacity presented a *prima facie* case for Community rationalization. I suggested calling a meeting of European industry ministers to discuss what could be done. He cut me short: 'You do not understand. The ministers are our enemies; they want to retain power in national hands. There is no point in exchanging views with people who are so deeply biased against us. Our task is to produce a European plan for shipbuilding which will be so utterly compelling that the people of Europe will press for its acceptance.' One could not help admiring the boldness of the approach, but in practical terms it was wholly counterproductive.

With this kind of leadership at the top, it came as no surprise that my department jumped with enthusiasm on every bandwagon that rolled by. The alleged misdeeds of transnational companies, the suspected abuse of power by the major oil companies at the time of the 1974 Arab-Israeli war, the need to regulate cross-border mergers and eurodollar markets – the department craved to be involved in them all; and their jealousy was thoroughly aroused when they discovered that an international monitoring job had instead been awarded to OECD or the United Nations!

What finally caused me to quit was the undisguised anti-Americanism of many of my officials. It was only after I had been in Brussels for a year that I discovered that Servan-Schreiber's much quoted book, *Le Défi américain*, had sprung largely from my department; the spirit of that tirade against alleged American imperialism still lingered in the corridors. There has always been a school of thought which holds that Europe can only get its economic act together by adopting a defensive and slightly hostile posture – Fortress Europe – towards the rest of the world. In early 1974 this view dominated our policies; and it was after taking part in a discussion in Spinelli's office about how to launch a largely vindictive anti-trust action against IBM that I took my decision to quit.

The Labour victory over Ted Heath in February 1974 gave me the pretext. As a more or less political appointee of the Heath government, I needed to give no other reason. My resignation was accepted for July and for most of the remaining five months I carried out a special assignment on energy for Henri Simonet, the Belgian commissioner. He was a most engaging man to work with and we became close friends.

Irritating as many of my Brussels experiences had been, the human relationships had always been congenial. One could not have wished for a more agreeable lot of colleagues or a more easygoing style of doing business. Instead of the stuffiness and intellectual arrogance one sometimes encounters in national bureaucracies, Brussels in those days had the air of a garrulous senior common-room where great – and mostly unrealizable – projects were tossed about with surprising nonchalance.

I developed a particular liking for Emil Noël, the brilliant French Secretary-General, who every Thursday gave us a run-down on what the Commissioners had discussed at their weekly conclave the previous day; it was like the head butler in a well-run country house briefing the staff on arrangements decreed by the head of the household. I also had enormous respect for the man who succeeded me, Fernand Braun from Luxembourg, and for Spinelli's Chef de Cabinet (now Braun's successor), Riccardo Peresich, both exceptionally gifted public servants.

Among the Commissioners – beyond the green baize door – I got on particularly well with François Ortoli, the former French Finance Minister, who was President of the Commission. In spite of the embarrassment my quixotic behaviour caused him, he and his wife gave us a charming farewell party to which they tactfully invited only those Commissioners with whom they knew I had not crossed swords.

Some memories spring to mind as I recall my Brussels assignment. Shortly after my arrival I had a visit from the

German organizer of what has now become the annual World Business Forum in Davos. My predecessor and his staff had evidently played a major role in these gatherings and the organizers were anxious that I should attend the 1974 session. I happen to have a deep aversion to conventions and conferences; and in order not to hurt feelings I decided on the silly excuse – which haunted me later – that my doctors thought the altitude of Davos would be bad for my blood pressure!

My relations with the press were always good, though *Private Eye* once dubbed me 'Eine kleine Ego-Kraut', a description which my family absolutely loved and which they wickedly suggested should have been the title of this book. But there was one occasion when the *Economist* inadvertently (at least I hope inadvertently) caused me a small drama. One of its reporters came to Brussels to interview me about the problems of the European shipbuilding industry, an outstanding candidate for rationalization. I was asked what my Directorate could do to slim it down. I told him that rationalization meant that some yard or yards would have to shut and that ultimately this boiled down to the question of which countries had to make the sacrifice.

To illustrate my point I added – off the record – that in recent UK history there had been two diametrically opposed approaches to this problem: that of Lord Beeching at the railways and that of Lord Robens at the coal mines. Beeching wrote and published a brilliant analysis of the railway problem, concluding that many of the services were unnecessary and that the workforce would have to be heavily reduced; there was an immediate uproar, leading to Beeching's resignation and years had to go by before the problem could be tackled. Robens, by contrast, went round the country making bullish statements about the future of coal in Britain, while quietly (and without a single strike) carrying out the biggest labour redundancy programme in history. Unfortunately, the *Economist* carried this little story with full attribution – and in a very conspicuous position – the following week; and the consequent uproar, including a one-day strike against me by shipyard workers in Genoa, reduced my relations with European trade unions to a very delicate state for months to come.

The fact that I had been appointed in an unusual manner caused me to be given a kind of eccentric's licence which in turn allowed me – or so I chose to believe – a freedom of behaviour and expression that I exploited to the full. I finally left Brussels in July 1974, sixteen months after my arrival. As a farewell present my colleagues gave me a puppet from the famous Belgian Théâtre des Marionettes; it would serve as a reminder, they said, both of Brussels and of my histrionic qualities!

11

Business as Usual

AS I ANTICIPATED, my active career had by then suffered too many interruptions to be easily resumed. I went on dabbling in my former activities without executive responsibility for any of them. It turned out to be an agreeable way of being involved in a variety of things and yet having time for my family and for the occasional excursion into public affairs.

I started with an office at General Electric but soon took one of my own a few blocks away. For a short time I became senior partner of a leading firm of London stockbrokers, Panmure Gordon (causing shock-waves by being the first ever to be admitted to Stock Exchange membership without passing the required examination). I also joined a number of corporate boards, including several (R.J. Reynolds, Chrysler, W. R. Grace) in the United States. In the early 80s, I took to spending part of each year in New York where my wife and I kept a small apartment and in Italy where we had our main home. (The Chianti wine we grew in our small vineyard acquired temporary notoriety thanks to a write-up by Kenneth Rose in the *Sunday Telegraph*.)

In late 1974 a delightful farce occurred over my becoming – or rather not becoming – the non-executive Chairman of ICL, Britain's leading computer company, then jointly controlled by Plessey and GEC. My appointment was about to be publicly announced when someone remembered that Her Majesty's government, by virtue of a major loan granted to the company some years earlier, had a right of veto over the chairman. The Socialist Minister of Industry at the time was Tony Wedgwood Benn, my old sparring partner at the IRC. Perceiving his chance to get his own back at me, he proceeded to veto my appointment on the aggressive ground that I was too closely associated with the opposition. I felt this accolade deserved to be made public but was talked out of it by my colleagues.

Soon after my return from Brussels – in the depth of the 1974–5 recession – I was asked by the Director of the National Economic Development Office (Neddy) to undertake a study of the ways Japanese, French and German companies raised capital in their markets and what lessons we in Britain could learn from these. There was much talk at the time of the inadequacy of the British system – Labour ministers had taken to speaking of an 'investors' strike' – and of the superiority of other ways of doing things. I relished the opportunity of exploding prevailing myths: to my mind the problem lay not in any defect of the system but in the nature of the policies pursued by Labour which scared investors and industrialists. Tinkering with institutional architecture was no remedy; and my report disappointed those in Whitehall who had hoped for a painless solution based on the practices of other countries.

This peculiarly British fondness for imported solutions surfaced again two years later when I gave evidence to a committee set up by Prime Minister Callaghan under the chairmanship of his predecessor Harold Wilson, to enquire into the general functioning of the City of London. All sorts of myths had developed in this country about the benefits which German industry was supposed to derive from its closeness to major banks: as if the presence on its boards of bankers, representing large shareholdings, somehow magically enabled the people running these businesses to be wiser and more efficient.

The truth of course is that German bank shareholdings are in almost every case the product of accidental happenings and hardly ever the result of deliberate decisions; and that bankers sit on boards first and foremost to make sure that as little as possible of the lucrative banking business of that client goes to competitors. In return for this customer loyalty, the banks let it be known that in the event of an unwanted take-over bid their holdings would protect the incumbent management; and this has acted as a powerful deterrent to would-be predators in the Federal Republic. That German industry has nevertheless been so astoundingly efficient is proof of the superior skills of its managers and has nothing to do with bank shareholdings or directorships.

A fascinating discovery I made was how touchy the powers-that-be were in those days to the merest suggestion that one knew of the existence, let alone the work, of Cabinet committees. Somehow these perfectly ordinary bodies, which we now know to be the source of all major decisions in Whitehall, were then shrouded in a primeval mist and any reference to them was sacrilege. I found this out the hard way by inserting a paragraph in my Neddy Report suggesting that a Cabinet committee might be established for the specific purpose of ensuring that economic policy decisions, especially fiscal ones, were more carefully screened for their impact on industry. My reward was a severe reprimand from a senior Treasury official in front of the Chancellor of the Exchequer: 'It is no part of Mr Grierson's business,' he intoned pompously, 'to speculate about the work of Cabinet committees.' I felt like a naughty child.

I also had an extraordinary experience with the so-called

Diamond Committee, headed by Lord Diamond, lately a Treasury Minister. Though its chief role was to investigate and report on inequalities of income, it had been given the additional mandate of looking into the effect of statutory dividend limitation, then in force, on the capital-raising prospects of British industry.

I was flabbergasted by the first question put to me by Lord Diamond: why were investors so concerned about dividends which were taxed at up to 98 per cent when they could just as easily live on realising capital gains taxed at only 30 per cent? The implication, coming from a Socialist politician, was that one should live on one's capital (for what else are capital gains in an inflationary context?) and that, at the precise moment when one needed money to spend, investors would conveniently line up to take one out of one's holdings at the right price. The question seemed to stand sound investing on its head and I had fun answering it; and, as the hearing was a public one, the press picked up the point the following day.

One minor public activity in which I became involved at the time was the Council of National Academic Awards to which Shirley Williams, then Secretary of State for Education, had appointed me in 1978. It turned out to be one of the most boring duties I ever assumed. The function of the Council was to validate degrees awarded by polytechnics and other university-type institutions which lacked the authority to do so on their own; we had to assess by regular visits whether the establishments in question were qualified to run the courses they offered.

Since our judgements were highly subjective – and to a large extent influenced by our equally subjective secretariat – I doubt that we did much for the cause of higher education in general. More specifically, I remember being appalled at the way colleges set up for the vital purpose of providing vocational training almost invariably tried to turn themselves into mini-

Oxfords; much of our time was taken up assessing honours courses in philosophy and social sciences.

Another educational escapade was an invitation from Lord Annan, then Principal of University College, London, to serve on a 'strategy committee' he was setting up to consider various options for the future. I agreed to serve and received two or three summonses to attend meetings, all subsequently cancelled due to unforeseen circumstances. After four years' 'service' without a single meeting, the Secretary of the College asked me if I was willing to accept a renewal of my mandate for a further four years. I drew Annan's attention to this little joke of which he was blissfully innocent and was allowed to retire.

Around that time I again became marginally involved in Tory party preparations for office. Margaret Thatcher had been elected leader and Keith Joseph was her principal lieutenant. I was asked whether I would help and was invited to attend meetings of the economic committee of the Shadow Cabinet in Mrs Thatcher's room at the House of Commons which gave me my first and impressive opportunity of seeing that remarkable politician at work.

Keith Joseph also asked whether I would undertake on the party's behalf a study of the extent to which differences in education and training affected the respective performances of British and French civil servants. I was sceptical of the premise on which the question rested. It seemed to me that the differences lay less in background and education than in political environment. I suggested to Joseph that before committing ourselves to the expense of a formal study we should explore the subject informally with recently retired senior British and French civil servants. He agreed to my suggestion, and a dinner was arranged at our London house in late 1975 which was attended, in addition to Joseph and myself, by Sir Otto Clark, who had recently retired as Permanent Secretary of the Ministry of Technology, and by Simon Nora, former Chef de Cabinet of the French Prime Minister. I started the discussion by saying that we on the British side were anxious to find out why French civil servants often seemed more skilled than their British counterparts when it came to deciding important economic issues. Simon Nora levelled the playing field by telling us that his French friends usually saw things precisely the other way round!

We took nuclear power as an example and quickly established that the processes by which decisions were reached were remarkably similar in the two countries. If variances existed in the degree of intimacy prevailing between business, government and academia, they were not a major factor; nor did the question of educational background play as big a role as is sometimes assumed. The real difference lay in the fact that in France, once a decision on, say, nuclear energy had been reached, it was immediately acted upon; in Britain by contrast a variety of considerations – fear of public opinion, Parliamentary questions, the likely reaction of the scientific lobby – could cause an essentially agreed decision to be delayed for years. In other words, whilst a deferential and *dirigiste* society such as France could swallow controversial decisions, our more open society found this harder; and neither the way public servants were educated nor the procedures of the bureaucracy had much to do with that. We decided not to pursue the idea of a formal study.

In late 1977 I was invited by the Royal Society for the Arts to deliver one of its annual Cantor lectures. The precise choice of subject was left to me but I was told it should be on the general topic of business and government. I worked hard on this lecture* and delivered it to a fairly full house at the Society's headquarters in March 1978. My text was an aggressive defence of private enterprise and I was not generous in what I

* See Appendix

had to say about bureaucracy. Several Whitehall mandarins were in the audience and, stung by what I said, used the question period after the lecture for a hard-hitting attack on my remarks.

Their intervention had a complex sequel. First, my lecture quite unexpectedly made the front pages of several newspapers next day; second, in an unprecedented fit of coyness the Royal Society, claiming that their recording machine had broken down, failed – for the first time ever – to reproduce the questions and answers in its quarterly bulletin, though it did print the actual lecture; and third – and most hilarious – the Permanent Secretary of the Department of Industry (making the point of my lecture for me) complained in writing to the managing director of GEC that it had been quite improper of me as Vice-Chairman of the Company to attack the very Whitehall department to which GEC owed so much!

In 1980 I also received an invitation from the Secretary-General of the Commonwealth to sit on a panel of experts to advise on an idea promoted at the recent Prime Ministers' conference in Melbourne. This idea, which struck me as fairly crazy from the start, was that the Commonwealth should establish a special bank to provide credit for exports from the thirty or so less affluent member countries. The considerable risk of loss would have fallen on Britain, Canada, Australia and New Zealand. We held a number of meetings at Marlborough House and I managed to persuade my fellow panelists that there was no chance of such a project being supported by the British Government and that we might as well say so in fairly plain terms. We did just that and no more was heard of the matter. But the experience gave me the opportunity of getting to know the Commonwealth secretariat, an amiable, bumbling – almost Pickwickian – outfit, languishing comfortably in Marlborough House. As a souvenir of my efforts, I still get each year a personal Christmas card from the Secretary-General.

Although more than five years had gone by since I left Brussels, the Commission crept back into my life in two guises. First, Stevie Davignon, then Commissioner for Industry, appointed me his 'special' adviser – for six months – with the specific task of criticizing the Commission's industrial policy. I wrote a paper casting doubt on the value of the Community's activism and making the point, subsequently developed by Lord Cockfield in the 1992 programme, that the implementation of the Common Market, i.e. the removal of remaining barriers so as to establish genuine Europe-wide competition, was by far the Community's best hope.

My other contact with Brussels, which I retain, is my chairmanship of the European Organisation for Research and Treatment of Cancer (EORTC). This body, which carries out cross-border clinical trials on new cancer-fighting drugs, is heavily supported both by the European Commission and the US National Cancer Institute. Thanks to a timely intervention by Jacques Attali in 1985 and the subsequent championship of our activities by President Mitterrand personally, it has now become the spearhead of the EC drive against cancer.

Although conferences are not my form, I thoroughly enjoyed two invitations – one to Vermont, the other to Aachen – from the Bilderberg Group, founded by Prince Bernhard of the Netherlands, which once a year brings together politicians, journalists and businessmen from NATO countries. I also attended several meetings of a similar body, the Trilateral Commission, chaired by David Rockefeller, but found their style more formal and less interesting.

One Trilateral meeting I shall never forget took place in Washington in the late 70s. Carter was President and, having previously as Governor of Georgia himself been a member of the Commission, he invited us to a gathering in the White House. We sat in horseshoe formation round his chair as he reminisced admiringly about the importance of the Commission. Waxing enthusiastic, he exclaimed: 'If the Trilateral Commission had existed in the 30s, we would not have had World War II.' This prompted my immediate neighbour, Paul Delouvrier, a cynical former French High Commissioner in Algeria, to whisper loudly to me: 'I can't somehow picture Hitler as a member of the Trilateral, can you?'

During the next few years my wife and I spent much time in the United States. As a result, my shoulder rubbing with Whitehall came to a temporary halt. It started again – I am sure for the last time – when Lord Gowrie, then Minister for the Arts, asked me in 1984 if I would take on the chairmanship of the South Bank arts complex due shortly to emerge as a semi-autonomous body from the passage of the bill then before Parliament for the abolition of the Greater London Council.

I had been involved with the arts for many years: most recently as Chairman of the Philharmonia Orchestra Trust and as board member of the North Carolina School of the Arts and the Phillips Collection in Washington. Becoming boss of a huge arts complex – the biggest in Europe – with the challenge of trying to improve it was hard to resist. It did not take me long to inform Gowrie that I was willing to serve.

12

The South Bank

THE OFFICIAL INVITATION came in November 1984. It required me to become a member of the Arts Council and to head a committee which eventually transformed itself into the semi-autonomous South Bank Board.

The bill abolishing the GLC had just had its first reading in the Commons. It was to transfer to the Arts Council not only ownership of the entire twenty-seven acres of riverside Lambeth loosely known as the South Bank but also administrative and artistic responsibility for those of its buildings and open spaces which were not, as for instance the National Theatre and the National Film Theatre, in the hands of tenants.

I accepted in full knowledge that I was taking on a vague and ill-defined task which would consume much of my time. As in the case of the IRC in 1966 – but in an even more controversial setting – an administration had to be created out of nothing to tackle a job which previously did not exist. But in contrast with the IRC, there was this time no shortage of candidates willing to serve; the problem was how to ensure an orderly and disciplined chain of command at the top without having to assume day-to-day management myself.

I was fortunate in quickly finding outstanding candidates for the two top functions, Richard Pulford for administration and Nicholas Snowman for artistic policy. As neither would take the job unless he could report directly to me, the Arts Council hit on the idea that I should temporarily become Executive Chairman, making the management team a troika instead of a tandem. This experiment worked splendidly during the six years of my chairmanship – twice as long as I had originally signed up for – and I believe our experience encouraged other arts bodies (and their Whitehall minders) to overcome their traditional reluctance to split top management functions among equals.

Our worst period was the first sixteen months: from the time of my appointment until the GLC finally went out of existence on 31 March 1986. That the GLC mandarins took their demise badly and fought vigorously to the end came as no surprise; nor was it astonishing that the bill had a stormy passage in both Houses of Parliament. But we were not ready for the massive campaign of abuse hurled at us as heirs to what the GLC clearly regarded as one of their prize possessions; nor did we expect the quality press to support this campaign with such gusto. (Of all unexpected quarters, the *Field* – a distinguished magazine which normally devotes its pages to quite different pursuits – published a major article by Miss Widdicombe rubbishing the Board, the staff and myself and predicting all sorts of dreadful happenings at the South Bank under our stewardship.)

Our biggest headache came from the GLC's refusal, even after the bill had received Royal Assent, to cooperate on the steps needed for a businesslike handover. This put us in the absurd position of having to assume responsibility for the smooth functioning of a huge arts complex on a date nine months hence without prior access either to information about the state of the buildings or to the budget required to run them. It was a nightmare situation, forcing us to recruit a shadow staff of some 180 people, including a complete shadow box office, and to award contracts for cleaning, security, etc., without being able to show applicants the physical spaces in which they were supposed to operate. Fortunately some brave members of the GLC staff ignored orders and gave us modest but welcome support; on the whole, however, we had to plan in the dark.

In the circumstances it was a miracle that we managed to move in on schedule, relatively unmolested except for the chaotic leftovers of a gigantic farewell party which it took an army of industrial cleaners wielding the latest state-of-the-art equipment several days to clean up. At the farewell feast, Ken Livingstone, the outgoing GLC leader, lamented the fact that the Festival Hall would now be run by 'third-rate merchant bankers', which drew a loud 'hear, hear' from Christopher Bishop, Managing Director of the Philharmonia Orchestra. One clearly has friends in unexpected places.

The next four and a half years were calm in comparison. The press, which had been so critical before, gave us a long and probably undeserved honeymoon; and both the government and the Arts Council behaved impeccably towards us. Our aims were modest: to take a firm grip on the administration, to make the place more user friendly and to try to enrich the somewhat dreary concert repertoire. We made ourselves felt in all three areas.

In retrospect, we probably let the Treasury off too lightly by accepting at the outset a level of funding lower than we might have obtained; and we proclaimed too aggressively our determination to meet annual cost increases from commercial income and sponsorship. As a result, the government made a saving of £9 million at our expense between 1986 and 1990; and we had the tough task of earning and raising this amount ourselves.

My six years at the South Bank prompt a few reflections. First, I confess to having become somewhat sceptical about the true value of the so-called arm's length principle in arts funding, especially where large recipients of state aid are concerned. Great as is my respect for the Arts Council, I cannot bring myself to believe that its ranks contain wisdom enabling it to distribute these large sums of money more intelligently than an Arts Ministry would; a large proportion tends in any event to be earmarked in advance.

My second reflection is the comforting one that there really is not a scrap of evidence for the fashionable and gloomy belief that arts organizations cannot be run on sound business lines. My dedicated staff consisted predominantly of men and women with non-business backgrounds. This never stood in the way of their running a cost-conscious, lean and income-oriented organization. Indeed, the vigour with which my top managers reacted to adverse circumstances would have done credit to any commercial concern and instead of whingeing about the inadequacy of public funding, they got on with the job of living within our means.

Fundraising – arguably the most soul-destroying occupation in the world – was another subject. Its chic new title 'development' suggests that one is spared the embarrassment of being a beggar; one now becomes a businessman marketing a 'product' said to confer huge commercial benefits on whoever buys it. There is some truth in this; but, when one considers the cut-throat competition that has broken out between opera houses, theatres, orchestras, ballet companies, concert halls, museums, stately homes and the rest – all knocking on the same doors time after time – it is hardly surprising that compassion fatigue has set in.

Almost the only profoundly controversial issue of my South Bank tenure was contemporary music. The tendency of the major South Bank orchestras has always been to play safe in their programming and to put on music which would attract the public. But our grant from the Arts Council required us to provide for the performance of what is elegantly described as 'challenging music', i.e. music by twentieth-century composers, to which the response of the public is not overwhelming. Half empty (sometimes more than half empty) houses create deficits; and these must be funded from public sources.

My own relationship with contemporary music has never been cosy; a lot of it passes way over my head. But I accepted the argument that it should be performed and backed my management in the confident knowledge that they applied high artistic standards to its implementation. Yet the thought that we were making substantial public grants to performances attracting only a small élite, while orchestras performing music which appealed to the general public were desperately short of cash, caused me some uneasiness; and I am relieved no longer to bear this controversial responsibility.

Finally, a philosophical reflection. I am by nature a thick-skinned cynic expecting the worst, but the brutality with which one is attacked in the arts world if one has the misfortune of taking one wrong turn makes the politics of other professions seem very friendly by comparison.

In the early summer of 1989 we suffered two small mishaps, both of short duration and neither of lasting consequence. We ran into an industrial dispute, causing the loss of one and a half working days, and we incurred a book, not a cash, deficit of £1 million. The former was eventually settled to the satisfaction of both sides. Steps to correct the latter were instantly and successfully taken; but not before we had a rare opportunity to find out who our friends were. The press, with one or two notable exceptions, quite clearly were not. One by one they came to inspect our rotting corpse; one by one they dismissed our assurances, accurate as things turned out, that there was nothing wrong that could not be speedily dealt with. Articles appeared about our 'beleaguered condition', our impending bankruptcy and the disintegration of our management. It was all rubbish and lasted the statutory four to five weeks, after which the press turned its attention elsewhere and left us alone. But the experience was fascinating.

Equally fascinating and more sinister was the reaction of other friends. Two of my distinguished board colleagues indulged in an English practice with which I had not previously been familiar. They 'put down markers' about more troubles to come and had them minuted, the object presumably being to be able to say 'I told you so' if things got worse. Luckily we had the situation firmly under control; but the incident made me aware of how innocently un-English my reactions still were.

To stir things up, Sir Neville Marriner, the conductor, when interviewed on Channel 4 about the competition for orchestral residency which we had launched, said that he could not imagine why anyone would want to be resident on the South Bank! And just in case not everybody was tuned in to Channel 4, he repeated the remark in an interview with *The Times* the following day. In the same vein, but somewhat more privately, the trustees of a well known family foundation, having previously all but promised us a sizeable gift, then withdrew because 'they did not like the smell of things on the South Bank'. And Mr Esa-Pekka Salonen, the distinguished Finnish musician and principal guest conductor of the Philharmonia, also speaking to *The Times*, flattered us by likening the South Bank administration to Stalinist Russia. Last but not least, the manager of one of London's major orchestras wrote a letter to the Chairman of the Lambeth Planning Committee, with whom our horns were then locked over a major planning application, formally and enthusiastically offering his orchestra's help to defeat it. In none of my previous and more important public incarnations had I encountered bitchiness and hysteria on quite this scale.

Yet, on the whole, my South Bank appointment gave me more satisfaction than either the IRC or Brussels. Thanks to an excellent staff, I was able to get things done instead of merely praying that no idiocies would be committed in my name; and a few months ago I was able to hand over the establishment to my successor in good running order.

Postscript

AS I APPROACH the 'sell-by' date of my active life, I sometimes wonder whether a more conventional career – one without interruptions – might have been more fulfilling. Not knowing what success I might have had, I rarely push this line of introspection too far.

Perhaps it was just coincidence, but the chops and changes in my career seemed to mirror a similar pattern in my earlier life. Uprooted from a German Gymnasium at the age of eleven, hardened for the next three years in a French Lycée, I entered public school in England at fifteen, university at eighteen, a British prison camp shortly after that and eventually the British Army for the whole of those impressionable years from nineteen to twenty-five which in normal circumstances serve as a base for prudent career planning.

The constant factor in my young days was an exceptionally happy and relaxed family life. Neither the migrations nor the accompanying language changes were ever traumatic; even in wartime, they took place against the background of a close relationship with my parents who provided sound advice and a comfortable home base. But easy acceptance of change was something I undoubtedly inherited from the pattern of my youth; and, while it does not specifically explain why I was drawn into so many dalliances with the public sector, the underlying restlessness must have owed something to it.

My family tells me that I am a mild workaholic. The truth is that I have always enjoyed everything I have done. This probably led to carelessness in drawing the line between work and leisure – the occasional 'spillage' of work into what should have been weekends or holidays – and my family and those who worked for me were the chief sufferers. Had they been less tolerant, my vigorous appetite for truancy would have been much more difficult to indulge.

The Mirage of the State's Entrepreneurial Role

Text of lecture delivered at The Royal Society of Arts on 13 March 1978

It is a contemporary fallacy that some natural identity exists between the responsibilities of government and those of business. This in turn leads to the belief that all would be well if only we had a government of businessmen. I myself have never been able to subscribe to this notion, for it seems to ignore the essential fact that the prime responsibility of government is to govern and that little is gained by a frantic search for a spurious resemblance to business.

Business managers have a clear objective – to satisfy a market; and profit is the measurement of their success in allocating resources wisely to that end. Government has no similarly clear objective. Its task in the economic field is to hold the ring between the many popular pressures, frequently irreconcilable, which assert themselves; to legislate and raise revenue for such social objectives as are from time to time held important; and generally to protect the weak from the strong. There is no way of measuring achievement in such diverse enterprises and every generation must decide for itself whether the restrictions thus imposed on its economic freedom are a proper price to pay for accomplishing these broader objectives.

What impact has this confrontation between business and government on the processes which create wealth? First, let us recognize that no democratically elected government could ever institute a perfect or flawless environment for private enterprise. Nothing so utopian is expected of it, nor indeed could two businessmen be found who would agree on exactly what such an environment ought to be.

Fortunately healthy private enterprise is able to survive and flourish even in the face of a considerable volume of government regulation. The first effects of regulation – and this is certainly true of taxation – tend to be adverse, but provided the laws and taxes enacted by the state leave a proper balance between penalties and incentives – and so long as the basic motivation of enterprise is not eroded – the wealth-creating processes do not find it impossible to surmount these obstacles.

The same cannot be said of the state's 'entrepreneurial role' if by that we mean that extra dimension of state activism which has in recent years been a feature of the British scene and which goes considerably beyond mere central direction or guidance of the economy. Its outstanding examples were of course the Industrial Reorganisation Corporation and the National Enterprise Board, but it would be quite wrong to think that state activism in the economic field stopped there. Indeed, for every pound of taxpayers' money committed by those two organizations, at least two pounds – and probably much more – were committed on similar promotions by the state itself.

In this role the state seeks to justify its activity with lofty claims that it is creating new wealth. These claims are rarely borne out by subsequent events and we thus have the curious paradox of regulatory intervention attempting to curb the power of business without much thought for wealth creation and yet not inflicting significant damage, while entrepreneurial intervention sets out with the specific object of increasing national wealth and almost invariably achieves the exact opposite.

When I became Head of the IRC in 1966, ministers and civil servants (and some of their friends on the IRC Board) were fond of referring to the IRC as a government merchant bank, free to venture its funds wherever it saw the chance of a profit. For my part I took pains to make it clear, both in public utterances and in discussions with Whitehall, that I rejected this view completely. For me the IRC was a financial standby of last resort and possibly a behind-the-scenes coordinator of certain initiatives in the world of industry; but nothing more.

Entrepreneurial government bestows its patronage selectively and at random. Under the banner of 'backing winners', ministers and civil servants fancy themselves as latter-day Carnegies or Rockefellers; and hundreds of millions of tax-payers' money are ventured on what Professor Jewkes once called 'headlong charges down frustrating cul de sacs.' 'Investing from the hip' would be another way of describing these remarkable adventures.

Naturally there are always takers for this kind of bountiful support. And it is equally not surprising that in such circumstances the powerful mandarins of Whitehall who ultimately rule our destinies come to develop a staunch belief in the indispensability of their patronage and in the value of the contribution which their own exertions make to national prosperity. The 'conceit of certainty' is very pervasive.

What is surprising is how rarely this conduct of government is challenged on practical grounds. Public scepticism seems more preoccupied with the theoretical foundations of state intervention, with its legitimacy in constitutional terms. Not that this is unimportant – the 'blacklist' revelations of recent weeks show all too clearly how vigilant one needs to be on that front. But the question really to be asked about the state as entrepreneur is not so much 'may the state do this?', but rather 'can one expect one iota of extra national wealth to be created by all this frantic busy-bodying?'

What invariably happens is that Whitehall becomes convinced that some important gap has developed in the wealth-creating process which only a state-financed promotion can fill. Thus the groundnut scheme of unhappy memory; the Concorde programme; the aluminium smelters of the late 1960s; the 'regeneration' of British Leyland in 1974–5; the rescue of Chrysler; the huge subsidy granted to obtain questionable shipbuilding contracts with Poland and India; and last, though not least, the underwriting – recently announced – of a tiny UK company's excessive trading commitment in Saudi Arabia. I am indebted to Mr Bernard Levin for reminding me in a recent article of that appropriate saying of Timon of Athens: ''Tis not enough to help the feeble up, but to support him after.'

One feature which distinguishes this kind of promotional activity from the more accepted regulatory function of the state is that the latter, even when pursued for such partisan ends as the redistribution of income or wealth, is on the whole governed by law, so that those administering it enjoy only limited discretion and that redress against abuse or malpractice is always available through the courts. By contrast, entrepreneurial intervention is wholly arbitrary and tends to depend on the whims and hunches of ministers and civil servants.

This arbitrariness is of course the essence of corporatism. But what exactly do we mean by that term? What is corporatism and what is the corporate state? One of the best definitions I have heard is that given by Lord Croham, the recently retired

Head of the Civil Service. He put it like this in a lecture to the London Business School in January, and I quote: 'Whenever there is a recognition that general objectives are desirable but have to be secured by agreement rather than by statute, the role of interest groups is bound to be important.' It would be hard to find a more apt description of the cosy private deals to which corporatism gives rise and which invariably go against the true national interest.

The prime justification for entrepreneurial intervention is usually declared by its advocates to lie in the alleged malfunctioning of the capitalistic market economy. 'The market is all right up to a point,' this doctrine proclaims, 'but the really important investment and financing decisions in the economy cannot nowadays be taken without that superior wisdom and those greater resources (meaning of course taxpayers' money) which only the state has at its disposal.' Such a view has the merit of making the state's entrepreneurship look virtuous and noble, but how realistic is it?

The expression 'capitalistic market economy' is a blend of two distinct phenomena. One of these, capitalism (by which I mean the capitalistic market, not private ownership) is not necessarily dependent on a free or market economy. It merely signifies the process by which men forego current consumption to save it for the future and which in turn permits these savings to be invested in capital resources. This process occurs in socialist as well as free economies, the main difference being that in a free society the saving is voluntary while under state capitalism it is coerced.

The market economy on the other hand is a very different proposition. It tends to exist only in free societies. Through its elaborate signalling system – flashing red, green and amber lights about changing consumer preferences, raw materials and other inputs – it becomes the ultimate arbiter of productive efficiency and hence of real wealth. Planned economies – that is coerced or guided ones – can build rockets, nuclear reactors and supersonic aircraft (though it has yet to be shown that they can also invent them) but the sum total of wealth to which their exertions give rise compares very unfavouraby with that of a free society. As Alfred Marshall put it one hundred years ago: 'A government could print a good edition of Shakespeare's works, but it could not get them written.'

What irks Whitehall is that the market economy cannot undertake to deliver a specific economic situation. Hence complaints about the failure of the 'free market system'. But market capitalism is not a system. Systems by definition are programmed ways of obtaining chosen results. The market economy, with its heavy dependence on trial and error, with its dispersed decision taking, its overlaps and its duplications, is of course nothing of the kind. The cardinal mistake made by central bureaucracies is to behave as if economic truths can be 'known', whereas in real life what passes for knowledge – for the purpose of deciding the 'best' way of producing the 'right' products – turns out to be primarily a matter of judgement or even guesswork.

I referred earlier to the unfortunate interaction – unfortunate in the sense that it stultifies the operation of the market economy – between the urge of the mandarins to patronize the economy and the readiness of substantial elements of the business community to submit to this patronage. One is reminded of Adam Smith's famous dictum that 'people of the same trade seldom meet together, even for merriment and diversion, but the conversation ends in a conspiracy against the public or in some contrivance to raise prices.'

With these words Adam Smith might have been describing any meeting of Neddy. For in spite of its Tory origins Neddy has become one of the arch-embodiments of the corporate state where the national interest is laboriously defined and where initiatives to implement it are launched on their ill-fated journeys.

Corporatism is the frame of mind in which producers, instead of facing the risks and penalties (and of course also the rewards) of the free market, huddle together in the bunkers of Whitehall and Millbank (and, until the recent change in top management, also in those of Tothill Street) and in the name of some mystical public interest try to 'rationalize' their relationships with each other and with the government of the day. I remember how in 1966, when I had just been appointed to run the Industrial Reorganisation Corporation, I received a visit from a distinguished American industrialist. After congratulating me on my new post, he cleared his throat and enquired in a rather timorous way – clearly wondering whether he was touching on a sensitive nerve – whether the British government's blessing of 'rationalization', implicit in the IRC White Paper, meant that in future cartels and cartel-like arrangements would cease to be frowned upon and might actually be approved. It then dawned on me that in the United States (and indeed in this country up to 1939), 'rationalization' was a cosmetic word for combinations in restraint of trade. Few businessmen reject the offer of such combinations if they are legal and it is only the sanction of a prison sentence, as in the United States, which deters their adoption. No wonder that the concept of the state collaborating in such helpful arrangements seemed almost too good to be true to my astonished American friend.

Yet that is what the corporate state and Neddy are about. For competition, with the accompanying penalties for failure, is not man's natural habitat. He accepts its disciplines only if and to the extent to which the rewards for success are correspondingly enticing. When these rewards cease to attract him the average businessman either opts out or seeks the safe anchorage of the corporate state and the cosy get-togethers of the world of Neddy and public patronage.

Whenever a particular industry comes under Neddy

scrutiny, the predictable discovery is that if only there were more collaboration and less competition, and if only the government would support – a convenient euphemism for 'subsidize' – certain unprofitable activities, that industry would dramatically improve its compliance with the national interest. If the national interest is deemed to lie in increased exports, Whitehall stimulates them by selective subsidies or guarantees; if the national interest is deemed to lie in shrinking an industry down to a single UK firm, incentives are offered to induce several firms to merge; if the national interest is deemed to lie in excess labour being absorbed in a development area, UK or foreign firms are financially enticed to build plants there; if the national interest is deemed to lie in a so-called incomes policy, government tries to bully firms which see things differently by threatening punitively to withhold public sector contracts, export guarantees or permission to raise insurance premiums. No unconstitutional monarch of the eighteenth century could have been more wilfully arbitrary.

What all such actions have in common, beside their subjective definition of the public interest, is a tendency to divide the business world into goodies and baddies. The goodies – generally, but not always for long, the bigger businesses – are those willing to collaborate. Others who choose to follow their own paths are ostracized. It was precisely on this issue of the arrogance of public judgements on private matters that I chose to resign from the IRC.

There is another issue which I find equally worrying. No one nowadays seriously questions the right of government to rescue industries in trouble when exceptional circumstances leave little alternative. If bodies like IRC and NEB confined themselves to such tasks, there would be little serious objection. But the new and trendier notion is that these bodies are on trial as moneymakers for the public purse; or, to put it more bluntly, that the state has a role as punter with public funds. This was a view much trumpeted by Lord Ryder when he announced that under his leadership the NEB would make a good profit on the money which the taxpayer had entrusted to it.

I cannot help feeling that this view is based on a fundamental misconception of the proper role of the state when confronted with an unavoidable entrepreneurial task. The state's duty on these occasions should be confined to ensuring, with the aid of the best advice available, that such public funds as are committed to a rescue are wisely husbanded and that the taxpayer ends up with the minimum loss. Obviously the taxpayer would rather end up with a profit than a loss, but profit making – as distinct from good husbandry – should never be a prime consideration in judging the effectiveness or success of state entrepreneurship.

The lurch towards the corporate state has gone almost to the point of no return, yet no one really wishes to admit this. Hence the popularity of the new jargon: 'mixed economy', 'pluralism', 'government–industry partnership' are all terms designed to obfuscate the issue. Whatever is implied by the expression 'mixed economy' – and there is some doubt whether it has a real meaning at all – it certainly does not imply that the metabolism of capitalism has changed and that its disciplines have become irrelevant.

The only relevant sense in which we now live in a 'mixed economy' is in the frighteningly large number of our enterprises which have been insulated by nationalization from the impact of these disciplines and are underwritten by the taxpayer against that most basic discipline of all – the risk of failure. For businesses still in the private sector – and they continue to represent the bulk of our economic activity – there has been no change in disciplines at all. On the contrary, the challenges of the contemporary economic scene call for greater vigilance than ever on the observance of these disciplines.

This elementary fact is sometimes overlooked by those who

try to draw artful distinctions between 'big' and 'small' businesses and to argue that, while small businesses may still be entrepreneurial, big ones have become institutional. By institutional they mean that these businesses no longer respond to the normal 'carrot-and-stick' stimuli of capitalism and can be safely run as if they were part of the national bureaucracy. Nothing could be further from the truth. The characteristic of any private business, big or small, remains as always that it can go bankrupt.

The fairly recent advent on the British scene of the magical expression 'mixed economy' was greeted with much acclaim. It was as if the conventional wisdom had suddenly ordered a truce in the war of slogans; henceforth our duty was 'to make the mixed economy work'. The idea of a truce, however temporary, is in principle admirable. It responds to a public mood and matches the gravity of the situation. But peaceful slogans devoid of significant meaning can be as dangerous as warlike ones and there are disturbing indications that under the banner of 'mixed economy' a great flight from reality is in progress.

For what is the 'mixed economy' really about? Is it simply a reminder that in a civilized society everyone must act responsibly and accept certain limitations on his or her freedom and that in this fundamental sense we are all deeply interdependent? If so, it is hardly a novel thought and certainly not an economic doctrine. Or is 'mixed economy' just a way of admonishing us that we must keep a stiff upper lip and stop grumbling about an administration which interferes with ever increasing foolishness in our economic lives and which expects the private sector uncomplainingly to bear the burden of a huge public sector that is itself conveniently shielded from the basic capitalistic discipline of having to make ends meet? If this is the meaning, it scarcely does more than turn the knife in a rather painful wound.

In fact, all attempts at defining 'mixed economy' turn out to be fairly sterile; and one is left with the uncomfortable feeling that it is in the diffusion of an atmosphere rather than in the imposition of new disciplines that the real force and impact of this new wisdom lie. The adjective 'mixed', like that other term 'coexistence', conveys a flavour of harmony, togetherness and absence of friction – as if problems once thought divisive and controversial have by a flash of enlightenment ceased to be so.

It is easy to see how powerfully such a vision appeals to those who for a variety of reasons find it hard to come to terms with the freedom and diversity of capitalistic enterprise. For capitalism, even in the minds of those well disposed towards it, has always had an aura of Old Testament severity, heavy with wrath and punishment; while, by contrast, the comforting expression 'mixed economy' indicates that a transformation has taken place, that capitalism is now in a New Testament phase of sweetness, compassion and light, and that instead of tiresome old disciplines, such as having to compete or earn a profit, there is now lofty consultation among assorted mandarins.

The concept of the 'mixed economy', with its tacit acceptance of the virtues of bureaucratic coordination, represents a convenient halfway house between all-out planning and old-fashioned *laissez faire*; and it appeals powerfully to civil servants on whose role it confers an additional importance. For the business of civil servants is to administer and their approach to economic problems is an essentially organizational one. Their world is one of questionnaires and blueprints – and their training leads them to value a spurious tidiness above almost everything. Indeed, to a conscientious civil servant there is something unacceptably untidy about the restless dynamism of private enterprise. This also is why civil servants have an easier and more natural relationship with large semi-institutionalized businesses than with the vast realm of medium-sized and smaller businesses which do not fit so conveniently into the official order of things.

This search for neat patterns corresponds to a deep natural yearning, but ignores the fact that a dynamic economic society cannot live on a static formula. While it is perfectly proper for human societies to strive for the highest attainable degree of stability in their affairs, the spice of private enterprise happens to lie in enriching disorder, in adventurous diversity and in restless searching for new commitments. If this notion is accepted, it follows that one cannot afford too much squeamishness about the occasional overlap or duplication or indeed the inevitable tragedy when a business bites the dust as the price of having made too many mistakes. Indeed, there is bound to be something incurably kaleidoscopic about the shape of industry, as demarcation boundaries between trades change and as newcomers offer their challenges to the established order.

This of course is not how the planners see it. For them there is always the latest 'discovery' which explains all previous shortcomings. As each such discovery emerges, the impression is spread that we need just one more great patriotic heave by all concerned and the millennium is bound to be upon us. The fact that the main consequence of each heave is to damage the driving forces of private enterprise still further has not so far curbed the energy of these enthusiasts.

The air is still thick with the slogans of the headlong rush for blueprints and patterns. Not so long ago, when I was at the IRC, 'industrial reorganization' was the great 'in' expression. All problems could be solved by tinkering with the structure of industry – as though industry was a piece of architecture. Fancy theoretical notions about the right shape and size of individual industries were floating around freely and some heavy and expensive blunders were committed in their name.

The next phase was the indictment of the so-called 'candy-floss industries' and their punishment through the Selective Employment Tax. What was wrong with Britain, according to this notion, was our encouragement of too many service trades and our neglect of the heavy industries.

When this had run its course, its successors turned out to be 'industrial strategy' and 'industrial regeneration'. Neither term has a particularly clear meaning, but the underlying concept is that wrong economic policies at the centre can be offset by tinkering here and there with individual industry groups.

Finally came the arch-slogan of all, coined by Sir Frederick Catherwood. What was really wrong with Britain, we were now told, was that bankers and investors had gone on strike. This should have been dismissed as a joke in bad taste. Instead a considerable effort has had to be devoted over the last three years to refuting this perfectly absurd notion which corresponds to no observable truth.

So powerful is the spell of the corporate state that we accept the concept of a so-called 'government–industry partnership' as though it were a pillar of our constitution. It is of course nothing of the kind. Indeed, constitutionally speaking, there can be no such thing as a special relationship between government and business. It is one of the great triumphs of corporatism that this anomaly passes relatively unnoticed.

For the business citizen, individual or corporate, is no different in status from any other citizen; and his relationship with the state should be governed by law (subject to proper constitutional safeguards) and nothing else. The forging of special links is a typical corporatist phenomenon and business-men who play this game ought to ask themselves whether they are really acting in their own best long-term interests.

It is a curious fact that really robust business communities tend to develop their own resistance to interfering governments. An interesting case in point is the relationship between business and government in the United States. In our great awe at the tremendous achievements of American industry we tend to forget that these achievements were won in the face of a gigantic populist onslaught, conveniently fed – it must be admitted – by the emergence of a number of major scandals. The result has been that for well over a century every conceivable obstacle has been placed in the way of American private enterprise, especially large private enterprise, and that both the intentions and the practices of corporate business have been impugned and vilified in a manner that has no equal in Europe, let alone Japan.

Yet American business has come to terms with this way of life. Indeed one suspects that its colossal vigour owes something to its trial by fire in successive battles with both Washington and public opinion. American business takes it for granted that in the process of managing a social order able to contain the dynamic of private enterprise government is bound to find itself in collision with individual business groups and even with business interests as a whole. It has been the triumph of American business to hold its own in this gladiatorial contest.

By contrast the British contemporary attitude appears remarkably supine. The role of the state as nanny or governess – and the feverish search for a consensus which in the nature of things cannot be a genuine one – has taken firmer root in these islands, notwithstanding their long tradition of rugged individualism, than anywhere else in the industrialized world. Our acceptance of corporatism is in this sense a self-inflicted injury.

It is sometimes said in defence of this attitude that we are doing no more than copying the practices of, say, Japan and France, where differences between state and business appear to be taken care of around conference tables. International comparisons are always perilous, if only because the grass usually seems greener in the next paddock. But in this case the conventional wisdom really makes a major error. The idea that other countries have found some magical formula for eliminating conflict between state and business is incredibly naïve. What happens in Japan and France and in certain other countries is that a determined business community knowing exactly what it wants – and, in the case of Japan, operating in a conveniently neo-tribal setting – has succeeded in pressing the resources of the state into its own service. The conditions for achieving such a result simply do not exist in a traditionally liberal society like Britain.

Those of us who live in open societies would do well to ponder this basic truth and cease hankering after the interventionist gimmicks of less open ones. There is no stimulus to business efficiency remotely comparable to that of open competition. Certainly no other factor played so important a role in creating the great wealth of the United States. Its dynamic makes all tinkerings by government appear pathetically feeble in comparison.

It is surprising how reluctant we are as a nation to recognize this truth. We comfort ourselves, for instance, with the belief that in Japan there is no real competition among major firms. In fact competition between them is intense, as the recent flood of bankruptcies witnesses only too clearly. Equally, we tend to underestimate the critical role played in German postwar economic recovery by Professor Erhardt's courageous decision to liberalize imports and thereby stimulate competition.

One could think of many other examples of competition demonstrating its superiority over government tinkering. It could be argued, for instance, that the moves made by successive Tory presidents of the Board of Trade in the late 50s and early 60s to curb restrictive practices of various kinds constituted a far more powerful agent of wealth creation than a host of interventions by Neddy or NEB. And what about the curious but significant fact that neither the United States nor West Germany, surely two of the most successful liberal economies in the West, even possess such an institution as a

Ministry of Industry? Politicians would do well to ponder that one.

Other solutions may be good for other countries, but it has always seemed to me that the creative genius of the British people in commerce and industry flourishes in almost exactly inverse proportion to the amount of central tutelage applied to it. Perhaps it is too much to hope that the corporatist trend can be reversed in one bound, but the objective to be aimed at is surely a massive withdrawal of the economic bureaucracy and a firm rejection of the belief that the man in Whitehall knows best.